# How to Discern and Expel Evil Spirits:

## A Classroom Approach

By

# Prophetess Mary J. Ogenaarekhua

# Endorsement

"From the beginning, God's heart has been about restoring His church and inspiring His people to do His work. In this exciting and pivotal time in the kingdom of God, He is speaking through mighty messengers like Prophetess Mary Ogenaarekhua to enlighten and empower His church.

**In How to Discern and Expel Evil Spirits,** Mary brings out the wisdom of God as a strong directive to deal with satan and his demons here and now. The contents clearly outline satan's plans, methods, legal rights and God's provisions to effectively seize and thwart those plans. God's warriors are mandated to lay hold of the authority God has placed in them.

This book will empower many for His work and give them victory over the kingdom of darkness. I believe God is using it to set many, many free— Glory, Hallelujah!"

**-Lynne Baker**

# Dedication

I dedicate this book to God the Father, God the Son and God the Holy Ghost. Lord God, You gave me the words to write in this book and I give you all the glory. As it is written in Psalms 68:11 so You have done concerning this book:

> **"The Lord gave the word: great was the company of those that published it."**

Father, it is a great honor to be a student in your classroom. You taught me the materials in this book in three nights and you made it possible for me to write the teaching manual that resulted in this book in less than two weeks! You are truly a great teacher and You are the best! Thanks for bringing more and more students into our classroom.

Thank You also for giving me To His Glory Publishing Company. You have made it a great company.

# How to Discern and Expel Evil Spirits:
# A Classroom Approach

**All scriptures are quoted from the King James Version of the Bible.**

**Published by To His Glory Publishing Company, Inc.**
**463 Dogwood Drive, NW**
**Lilburn, GA  30047**
**(770) 458-7947**
**www.tohisglorypublishing.com**
**www.maryjministries.org**

**Book is available at:**
**Amazon.com, BarnesandNoble.com, Borders.com, Booksamillion.com etc.**
**www.tohisglorypublishing.com**
**(770) 458-7947**

*Cover designed by: Obasi Scott*

**International Standard Book Number: 0-9749802-8-5**

# Foreword

In a world where evil spirits are not recognized as evil, we as Christians must learn how to discern and expel them. The media and entertainment worlds have fed all who would eat large doses of Satan's lies and these lies have dulled our spiritual sensitivity. However, we cannot completely blame any sector other than ourselves for this. Therefore, we must return to what the Word of God says concerning evil spirits.

A large part of Jesus' earthly ministry involved discerning evil spirits and casting them out. We see this in the following biblical examples: Jesus casting out the legion spirits from the demoniac in **Mark 5:2-15**, His healing of the lunatic boy possessed with a devil in **Matthew 17:14-21**, His healing of the woman of Canaan's daughter who was vexed with a devil in **Matthew 15:22-28**, etc.

Prophet Mary O. is a promoter and defender of God's truth. Mary also has a heart for God's people to rise up in freedom and wholeness to fulfill their destiny. The foundation of **"How To Discern and Expel Evil Spirits"** is solidly based and stated on biblical facts. The activations and discussions in the book bring the facts into reality for the students.

In every activation section, the following goal is stated: **"The goal of the discussions is to teach the students how to recognize the activities of** evil spirits." This direction is also given, **"Be sure to highlight their evil patterns in each encounter discussed."**

Mary has given us a tool to teach about evil spirits and to learn how to cast them out as well as a challenge to live in the truth that makes us free— "Ye shall know the truth and the truth shall MAKE you free" **(John 8:32).**

**-Apostle Buddy and Prophet Mary Crum**
**Life Center Ministries, Dunwoody, GA**

# Table of Contents

# Preface

By God's grace, I have taken it upon myself to write down some of the principles that He taught me concerning discernment, spirit beings and walking in the realm of the spirit. So many people in Christendom have little or no knowledge at all concerning what goes on in the spiritual realm. As a result, they are not able to fight off the enemy of their soul who is out to steal, kill and destroy every human being.

My hope is that people's spiritual "eyes of understanding will be enlightened" as they study the principles outlined in this book. It is designed to help the reader understand the **key principles about discerning of spirits**, the **origin of evil spirits**, the **activities of evil spirits, how to identify evil spirits** and **how to expel evil spirits**. I also answered one of the most frequently asked questions in the body of Christ today, **"Can a Christian Have a Demon?"**

It is my hope and desire that by the time an average person goes through the teachings outlined in this book, he or she will no longer be ignorant about evil spirits and about spiritual matters.

I therefore, encourage you to take the Chapters in this book seriously and make a determination to apprehend the principles outlined in each Chapter. May the Lord give you great revelation as you read.

**Note:** *This book is from an actual classroom teaching. It is designed to give the reader the sense of sitting in the Discerning of Spirits Class. The discussions are real life classroom discussions and the topics are based on actual occurrences.*

# Acknowledgements

I want to thank all the **students in the Visions and Dreams Class** for encouraging me to develop the teachings in this book. You all are great students and I love you.

Lynne Baker, thank you for your support and encouragement also. You edited the very first draft of this book and for this I am very grateful.

Thanks Carolyn Bennett for also encouraging me to teach on discernment.

Thanks to the Life Center Ministries' Senior Pastors; Apostle Buddy and Prophet Mary Crum and the Assistant Pastors, Sam and Laura Lee Rose for giving me a venue to teach.

Thank you Janice Walker for helping me to type the lessons in this book. May God richly bless you.

Thanks Obasi for the work on the cover.

# Frequently Asked Questions

- Are evil spirits and unclean spirits the same as demons?

- Are evil spirits or demons the fallen angels?

- Are sicknesses and diseases the works of evil spirits?

- Can a Christian have a demon or an evil spirit?

- Do evil spirits truly roam the earth?

- Does the devil truly exist?

- How can you identify demonic activities?

- How do you stay delivered after the evil spirits are cast out?

- How do you war against them?

- What are evil spirits?

- What are their activities?

- Who is most likely to have a demon or an evil spirit?

# Chapter 1

# Key Principles About Discerning of Spirits

**Overview:**

If you have been moving in the deliverance or in the prophetic ministry long enough, you probably have experienced people coming up to you and asking you questions such as "Do evil spirits really exist?" "What are evil spirits?" "Do evil spirits truly roam the earth?" "Are evil spirits or demons the fallen angels?" "Are evil spirits and unclean spirits the same as demons?" "What are their activities?" "How can you identify demonic activities?" "How do you war against them?" "Are sicknesses and diseases the work of evil spirits?" "Who is most likely to have a demon or an evil spirit?" "How do you stay delivered after the evil sprits are cast out?"

These are some of the questions people will ask you. Then you have the one that most Christians want an answer to– "Can a Christian Have a Demon?" This is a popular question and some Christians in their good intentions get offended when they are told that a Christian has a demon because someone had taught them that a Christian cannot have a demon and also because they know that our human spirit was renewed when they got born again. Therefore, they will fight you and debate you in their effort to prove that a Christian cannot have a demon. By the time we come to Chapter 4, you should have a

19

good response for anyone that will ask you the question, "Can a Christian Have a Demon?"

My mandate from the Lord is to help you to be spiritually aware of the activities of evil spirits. You are to know who they are, what they do, how they do what they do, how you can identify them and how you can cast them out. The purpose of this book is to teach you how you can really walk victorious as a Christian and how you help others live a victorious Christian life. God wants you to have victory not only in your life but also in your family and in places you go. He wants you to be able to walk into a place and sense any demonic activity going on there and to know what to do. My goal in this Chapter is to lay the foundation that evil spirits exist.

**Discernment is a Gift from God:**
When we talk about discerning of spirits, we quickly have to establish the fact that the ability to discern spirits (good or bad spirits) is not something that just happens to somebody, there is a reason why we as born again Christians are able to do this.
 I Corinthians 12:8-10 tells us why:

> *[8]For to one is given by the Spirit the word of wisdom; to another the word of knowledge by the same Spirit; [9]To another faith by the same Spirit; to another the gifts of healing by the same Spirit; [10]To another the working of miracles; to another prophecy; to another discerning of spirits; to another divers kinds of tongues; to another the interpretation of*

20

*tongues: [11]But all these worketh that one and the selfsame Spirit, dividing to every man severally as he will.*

I emphasize that it is God that gives us spiritual gifts as we have just read in the above scripture and as we noted that to one is given by the Spirit, the word of wisdom, to another the word of knowledge by the same spirit, to another faith by the same spirit, to another the gift of healing by the same spirit, to another the working of miracles, to another prophecy and **to another discerning of spirits.** This is the one we are interested in. It is not everybody in the world that can discern spirits. It is not even every Christian that can discern spirits. You might meet people who are into things that are diabolical and they tell you, "Oh I can see and do ...", but if they are not Christians, you know by what spirit they are operating. But for you to truly be able to discern the good spirits from the bad spirits, you have got to have the Holy Ghost. Discernment is a gift that God gives us when we are born again so that we can distinguish the good spirits from the bad spirits.

The discernment that we get from the Holy Ghost is the only one that we must accept. All others are counterfeit and we must reject them. You see from the above scriptures that God wants us to be able to operate with wisdom and discernment in this world. But before we can go into discerning of spirits parse, there are a few things that we must realize, because if you're going to speak on a subject you need to have a basic understanding of what that subject is. We're talking about spirits and we're talking about discernment. So it is in our best interest to know what a **spirit** is and what we mean by **discernment**.

**Spirit Defined:**
The dictionary defines a spirit as **"a supernatural being or the force that lives within living beings."** A spirit can be good or it can be bad or evil. We know that God is a Spirit— a good Spirit. Another definition of spirit is that **a spirit is a divine being.** It is something that transcends this present dimension that we are in. Therefore, when we are talking about seeing or discerning a spirit, **we are actually talking about being able to look beyond the earthly realm into the supernatural realm and perceive what is going on in that realm.**

In essence, discernment is all about seeing. Again, to be able to discern, you have to know what you're discerning. But in this particular case we're trying to discern spirits. If you look at **Jeremiah 29:11,** God tells us about His thoughts towards us:

> [11]**For I know the thoughts that I think toward you, saith the LORD, thoughts of peace, and not of evil, to give you an expected end.**

I told you before that God is the good Spirit as we learned and if you look in **John 4:24**, you will see that it is written—God is a Spirit.

**[24]God is spirit, and his worshipers must worship in spirit and in truth.**

These scriptures back up what I said before that God is the good Spirit, because when we talk about discernment, we are talking about being able to discern between the good spirit and the bad or evil spirit. God is the Spirit that has our best interest at heart and He is the Spirit that wants to do something good for us. But if you look at **John 8:44,** you see the Lord telling us about another type of spirit—the bad spirit.

**[44]Ye are of your father the devil, and the lusts of your father ye will do. <u>He was a murderer from the beginning, and abode not in the truth, because there is no truth in him</u>. When he speaketh a lie, he speaketh of his own: for he is a liar, and the father of it.**

This passage speaks of the fact that the devil is an evil spirit. For God and His angels are good but the devil and his evil spirits are bad. And Jesus gives us a clue as to the nature of the devil. **He was a murderer from the beginning and abode not in the truth because there is no truth in him. When he speaketh a lie, he speaketh of his own for he is a liar and the father of it.** So right there, when we say that the devil is bad, Jesus backs us up.

And furthermore, John tells us in **John 10:10** that:

**[10]The <u>thief cometh not, but for to steal, and to kill, and to destroy</u>: I am come that they might have life, and that they might have it more abundantly.**

This is one of the reasons why we must be able to discern the good spirits from the bad spirits because the good spirits are out to do us good but the evil spirits are out to kill us.  Therefore, we have to be able to tell which is which. And I say to you that God is operating a kingdom through our Lord Jesus Christ and His church.  At the same time, the devil is also operating a kingdom through the world system using evil spirits.  These evil spirits that rebelled along with Lucifer are "disembodied spirits."  In others words, evil spirits are spirits that were stripped of their terrestrial bodies.  They no longer have physical bodies on earth to move about and this is the reason why we cannot see them.  God stripped them of their terrestrial bodies so they are now what we call "disembodied spirits." They just float around looking for human bodies to live in.  These evil spirits are known as demons. This will answers the question – Are evil spirits and unclean spirits the same as demons or devils?  The answer is "yes".  These evil spirits are called demons, devils, principalities, powers, rulers of the darkness of this world and spiritual wickedness in the heavenly places because they are out to do evil all the time.

Look at **Ephesians 6:12**:

**¹²For we wrestle not against flesh and blood, but against principalities, against powers, against the rulers of the darkness of this world, against spiritual wickedness in high places.**

This scripture really gives us a good picture of evil spirits and our dealings with them. It says, "For we wrestle not against flesh and blood but against principalities, against powers, against rulers of the darkness of this world, against spiritual wickedness in high places." Because these evil spirits lack terrestrial bodies and they can no longer operate on earth without human bodies, they are out and about looking for human bodies. Do you see why we must discern them? We do not want them to inhabit our families or us. They need human bodies so that they can express themselves through these human bodies. But I will discuss this in detail when I go into the origin of evil spirits in Chapter 2.

**Discernment Defined:**
Earlier on, I touched briefly on discernment but we need to be well grounded on the definition of discernment. **To discern something means to perceive, to look into another dimension from this dimension and be able to tell by the Holy Spirit what is going on in that dimension. In other words, discernment is the ability to see things that are hidden, things that are obscure to the normal eye.** By the eye of the Spirit we can perceive something in another dimension. This is why somebody that has

25

the Holy Spirit can come up to you and say I saw this and that over you. Let us pray in order to break it off you – there's something, maybe an assignment against you, which needs to be destroyed.

**Evil Spirits Exist:**
We have established the fact that the good Spirits are God and His angels. The bad spirits are the devil and his demons. There are people that do not want anyone to talk about spirits and they say, "You Christians are always talking about demons and evil spirits or clean spirits, where do you come off?" Well, we know that God made this world and that the Word of God is truth and it tells us that evil spirits exist. Jesus prayed to God the father in **John 17:17** to:

> [17]**Sanctify them by the truth; your word is truth.**

The Word of God is truth and we are not afraid to discuss what we believe about it. It commands us to cast out evil spirits and to enforce the Kingdom of God on earth – that's our job. So do not be shy when the subject of evil spirits comes up and do not let anyone get you to back down because we know from the Word of God and from our encounter with evil spirits that demons are real. Actually, the people most afflicted by evil spirits are the ones that will tell you that demons do not exist and when you look at them, you can see the demon in their faces.

That is why I tell you right now that because

we wrestle against evil spirits, it is not in a person's best interest to stubbornly believe that evil spirits or demons do not exist. Actually, the devil wants you to believe that him and his evil spirits do not exist. This way, he can reign and prosper in his evil ways in your life without any interference.

I want to give you more scripture or background on the existence of evil spirits. Look at **Deuteronomy 32:17**:

> *17 They <u>sacrificed to demons</u>, which are not God— gods they had not known, gods that recently appeared, gods your fathers did not fear.*

God is talking about the children of Israel and how they offer sacrifice to gods whom they knew not, to new gods (devils) that came newly up and whom their fathers feared not. The problem of demons existed even as far back as the Old Testament days of Moses.

Also look at **Psalms 106:37**:

> **Yea, they sacrificed their sons and their daughters <u>unto devils</u>...**

I tell you that if the Bible acknowledges the existence of devils, you as a Christian had better also believe that they exist. It is detrimental for a Christian to believe that devils or evil spirits do not exist.

*Historical Account of the existence of demons:*
The Jewish historian named Flavius Josephus wrote about the existence of demons. He was a secular historian; he was not even a Christian. He wrote many books and parts of the books are called **"The Jewish War."** In **Chapter 6 verse 3**, he talked about a certain type of medication. Look at what he said the purpose of the medication was:

...It quickly drives away those called demons, which are no other than spirits of the wicked that enter into men that are alive and kill them unless they can obtain some kind of remedy against them.

This is someone who was not even a Christian. He was just an historian but he wrote about the demonic activities going on in his society in his days **and he called the spirits demons.** He also outlined the working of these spirits by telling us that these demons enter into people and they try to kill the people, unless the people can gain some kind of victory over them. As for us, we want to be armed and dangerous against these spirits so that they do not enter us to kill us.

Also, we learn in **I Samuel 16:14** that an evil spirit tormented King Saul after he disobeyed God, and this is how it is recorded:

**But the Spirit of the Lord departed from Saul, and an evil spirit from the Lord troubled him.**

When the Spirit of the Lord departed from King Saul, an evil spirit began to torment him. King Saul picked up the spirit when he consulted with a witch and God just allowed the spirit to torment him.

**Jesus Confronted Evil Spirits:**
Always remember that the Lord Jesus spent a great deal of his ministry time in casting out devils or unclean spirits. Evil spirits were a reality in the world in which He lived and they are a reality in the world in which we now live. **Mark 5:2** shows us an example of the Lord Jesus' encounter with an evil spirit.

> **²And when he was come out of the ship, immediately there met him out of the tombs a man with an <u>unclean spirit</u>...**

The emphasis is on the unclean spirit, and I am still establishing the fact that demons or evil spirits exist and that Jesus dealt with them. Therefore, we should not be afraid to deal with them. The scripture continues thus:

> *³Who had his dwelling among the tombs; and no man could bind him, no, not with chains: ⁴Because that he had been often bound with fetters and chains, and the chains had been plucked asunder by him, and the fetters broken in pieces: neither could any man tame him. ⁵And always, night and day, he was in the mountains, and in*

29

*the tombs, crying, and cutting himself with stones. [6]But when he saw Jesus afar off, he ran and worshipped him, [7]And cried with a loud voice, and said, What have I to do with thee, Jesus, thou Son of the most high God? I adjure thee by God, that thou torment me not.[8]For he said unto him, Come out of the man, <u>thou unclean spirit.</u> [9]And he asked him, What is thy name? And he answered, saying, My name is Legion: for we are many. [10]And he besought him much that he would not send them away out of the country.*

Demons like their territory or places of habitation. They will fight a person to keep their house because human bodies are the places they like to inhabit. So, if they have to use a false doctrine that tells you they don't exist to hold you down so that they can continue to live in you, they will. The scripture continued thus:

*[11]Now there was there nigh unto the mountains a great herd of swine feeding.[12]And all the devils besought him, saying, Send us into the swine, that we may enter into them. [13]And forthwith Jesus gave them leave. And the unclean spirits went out, and entered into the swine: and the herd ran violently down a steep place into the sea, (they were about two thousand;) and were choked in the sea.[14]And they that fed the swine fled, and told it in the city, and in the country. And they went out to see what it was that was done. [15]And they come to Jesus, <u>and see</u>*

*__him that was possessed with the devil, and__*
*__had the legion, sitting, and clothed, and in__*
*__his right mind__: and they were afraid.*

When you start casting out devils, people get afraid. Some people will speak against you because the demons in them will get agitated and will use the people to try to give you a bad reputation. Why? So that they can keep away more people from your deliverance meetings. But we know what the devil's tactics are and we also know to whom we belong and what power has been given to us.

For further illustration of the ministry of Jesus and His encounters with demons, let us look at **Matthew 8:16**:

*[16]When the even was come, __they brought__*
*__unto him many that were possessed with__*
*__devils: and he cast out the spirits with his__*
*__word__, and healed all that were sick:*

Again, the scriptures below show us that Jesus our Commander in Chief confronted evil spirits. We read another account of His encounter with evil spirits in **Matthew 15:22-28**:

*[22]And, behold, a woman of Canaan came*
*out of the same coasts, and cried unto him,*
*saying, Have mercy on me, O Lord, thou*
*son of David; __my daughter is grievously__*
*__vexed with a devil__. [23]But he answered her*
*not a word. And his disciples came and*
*besought him, saying, Send her away; for*

31

*she crieth after us. <sup>24</sup>But he answered and
said, I am not sent but unto the lost sheep
of the house of Israel. <sup>25</sup>Then came she and
worshipped him, saying, Lord, help me.
<sup>26</sup>But he answered and said, It is not meet
to take the children's bread, and to cast it
to dogs. <sup>27</sup>And she said, Truth, Lord: yet the
dogs eat of the crumbs which fall from their
masters' table. <sup>28</sup>Then Jesus answered and
said unto her, O woman, great is thy faith:
be it unto thee even as thou wilt.*

Pay attention because, this is where I was outlining
the above scriptures to get to:

*And her daughter was made whole from that
very hour.*

So we know now that:
(i) Not only do demons exist, not only do they inhabit
people, the Word of God has the power to get rid of
them. That same hour that Jesus spoke, those demons
were gone.

(ii) You cannot ever let anybody tell you that demons
do not exist. Whoever is telling you that demons do
not exist has the demons in him or her and that is
why they can say that.

If you look at **Matthew 10:8**, you will see
that the Lord Jesus gave his disciples authority over
evil spirits, and that He commanded them to cast out
evil spirits. What He said to them is applicable to

32

every single one of us and every single person who is born again. He commissioned them as they were going saying:

> *⁸Heal the sick, cleanse the lepers, raise the dead, <u>cast out devils</u>: freely ye have received, freely give.*

It is a direct command from our Commander in Chief that we go out there, not only to heal the sick, raise the dead, and cleanse the lepers but **to cast out devils** as well. So if Jesus believed that demons exist, we must also believe that they exist. And we are not going to be overrun by evil spirits but we will over-run them. We are to run them out of everyplace we go.

Looks also at **Acts 19:11-12** which tell us about how God used Paul:

> *¹¹And God wrought special miracles by the hands of Paul: ¹²So that from his body were brought unto the sick handkerchiefs or aprons, and the diseases departed from them, <u>and the evil spirits went out of them</u>.*

They took handkerchiefs that Paul was just using to wipe his face and when they touched somebody that was demon possessed, the evil spirits screamed and fled from the person.

**Example of How Evil Spirits Tried to Prevent My**

33

**Salvation:**

For years, nobody could preach the Gospel to me to get me saved. It did not matter what you said, I had a counter argument because God gave me a very bright mind. There was no way you were going to tell me a spiritual truth or occurrence that I did not have a logical explanation for. So, for many years, I could not get saved. But one day, I was sitting in church with my mom, and she got really sad because here she was in this ministry and in leadership but she has a daughter that cares nothing about what goes on in the church. I was just there to get her off my back. One day, one of the ushers came up to me and said, "Don't you think it's about time you gave your life to Christ?" And I said, "Is it by force?" And he said "No." And so I said, "OK, so get off my back." I then turned around and looked at my mom and it looked like she had lost everything that was valuable in life. She was looking very miserable so I answered the alter call but the Pastor did not pray for us to get saved. I want to say to all Pastors, please, pray for the people while you have them. Do not send them to some other place because you might lose some of them. They almost lost me in that process.

We were taken out of the sanctuary into another room. When I got into the room, I was assigned to a lady to talk to me. *At this time, I did not know that I was demon possessed but I was well dressed and I was looking good!* The lady I was assigned to said to me, "Oh, after I finish praying for you, you're going to become a saint." You never say that to a Roman Catholic person because the way we were taught about becoming a saint when I was a Catholic is that for you to be a saint, you have to have lived and died. After 200 years, the Pope tells them to dig up your bones and they will then pronounce you a saint after examining all your good deeds. To my knowledge, that was how they made saints. Therefore, I found it absurd for the lady to tell me that she was going to make me a saint! I looked at her and said: "You make me a saint? You?" She said, "yes." (*God is really laughing now because He remembers that incident!*) I said, "I am sorry, I am sorry for you and I am sorry for whoever has been putting those ideas in your head that you can make someone a saint, but I think I'm in the wrong place!" So I turned around and was about to walk off and she said, "You're not going to pray to receive salvation?" And I said, "Not if you're going to make me a saint!" She asked me, "You're leaving?" And I said, "Watch me!"

I could still see this lady and her desperation to get through to me that I needed to get saved. She did not want to grab me because it would appear too forceful. She did not know how to get it into my "demon-laden head" at that time that I needed salvation; that I was barely making it. Not knowing what else to do, she ran after me as I was about to leave the room and I looked at her and I saw that she was very concerned about me as though I was going to drop dead the next minute. She said to me, "Well, since you don't want to get saved, can I pray for you?" And

I said, "Of course." Roman Catholics always go to get prayed for so I did not mind her praying for me as long as she did not try to make me a saint. She took my hands and she prayed for me.

When I got back into the sanctuary, my mom asked me, "Did you get saved?" I said, "No, because the lady did not know how to make a saint. Why would I let somebody who is ignorant about how someone becomes a saint get me saved." She said, "You didn't get saved? I said, "No." This happened at the Sunday service. Do you know that the Tuesday of that week I got saved?

And this particular time as I stated in my book, _Unveiling the God-Mother_, I was about to come back to the United States and my mom said, "Go say goodbye to the Pastor." I was glad because I had wanted to talk to the Pastor about taking 10% tithes from my mom. I had an issue with that and I wanted to tell him to lay off my mom's 10%. Therefore, I was very glad at the opportunity to set him straight. So I went to the meeting all armed to fight this Pastor. When he opened the door, I heard a voice say, "peace be still." Whatever rage I came in with just went away and he began to talk to me. For the first time in my life, somebody was making sense with something that had to do with the Bible or with religion. And I sat there and listened. I got saved at this meeting with the Pastor just two days after my encounter with the lady. The Lord said to me years later:

**"Do you know what happened to you? Those demons had their fingers plugged into your ears. Nothing anybody said to you could get in. But when you allowed that spirit filled lady to touch you, you made contact with the Holy Spirit and the demons fled."**

That lady was the first spirit-filled person that I ever truly made contact with and received a blessing from. It was just a brief encounter and a blessing but I received it.

I said all that to tell you that just in line with the handkerchiefs coming out of Paul's body, when you make contact with unbelievers, it does good things for them; not just brushing against someone because I was living in the same house with my mom, but I was not receiving what she had to say. But this other lady, I received the blessing she prayed over me. According to the Lord, when I willingly made that contact with her, the demons fled and I got saved two days later. She was critical to my salvation, because otherwise I would not have been saved.

**Evil Spirits Are Subject to Christians:**
God has given us the direct command to go out there and cast out devils and to heal the sick. Scriptures tell us that demons exist and Jesus believed in their existence and He dealt with them. We are to believe they exist; we do not believe in them but we believe

they exist. Why? The reason is because we have a mandate from God to destroy them and their works. And this is what the Lord told us in **Luke 10:19-20:**

> *[19]Behold, I give unto you power to tread on serpents and scorpions, and over all the power of the enemy: and nothing shall by any means hurt you. [20]Notwithstanding in this rejoice not, that the spirits are subject unto you; but rather rejoice, because your names are written in heaven.*

Right there, we find out that God Himself has made evil spirits, demons, unclean spirits, and devils, however you call them – He has made them subject to us. Therefore, we are not to fear them. After reading this book, you should be able to use the biblical references to teach people that evil spirits exist. You should also be able to tell them that Jesus dealt with evil spirits. The Bible talks about their existence. Even a secular historian talked about their existence. We have been given a direct command to have dominion over them.

Sometimes I hear some fearful Christians telling other Christians, "Oh be careful what territory you go to make war in because you have to know what territory you have been assigned." Listen, we have been given authority to tread on serpents and scorpions. God did not put any limitation on us. We are to claim everyplace we tread spiritually. **We wrestle not against flesh and blood, but against principalities, powers in the heavenlies**. Therefore, do not let somebody tell you that you are not capable

38

of confronting evil spirits and do not become afraid to go downtown to do spiritual warfare because the devil might get angry. The devil is already angry. You know that he was rejected and we were created by God to replace him. You do not really have to do anything more to make the devil angry. Your very existence is enough to make him angry because he lost his position.

## Questions and Answers

**Question #1:** *I was talking to someone about Christmas yesterday and I was trying to explain why we shouldn't get into the spirit of Christmas and I could not get through to the person. Can you explain?*

**Mary's Answer:** **Maybe the person is like the way I was—with fingers in their ears! In terms of Christmas, for those of you who don't know me, I don't celebrate Christmas. A lot of people love their Christmas. I leave them alone at Christmas time. You know what I do when people are going about planning for Christmas? I write a book. When people are out there celebrating Christmas, I find something to write about. Christmas is a pagan feast because Christmas is not the same as the birthday of the Lord. The Lord's birthday you can celebrate, but Christmas you can leave to the pagans.**

**Christmas means "Christ-Mass." Mithra** (sun god) **worshippers celebrate the mass, which**

is where the celebration of Mass came into the Catholic Church. The Roman Catholic Church absolved a lot of the Mithra worship traditions. That's why you see the Nuns and the Priest not being married. These things are Mitra traditions as well as the exchange of gifts at Christmas. These are the things that Mithra worshippers do.

Also, when Constantine became a Christian, he was not a Bible believing Christian. He just had a dream in which he was told to fight by the cross and he accepted Jesus Christ but he did not really bothered to look in the Bible. As the Emperor of Rome, he just wanted his subjects (Christians and pagans) to get along. Prior to his time, Christians were being fed to lions and they were being persecuted and they were being killed. Christianity was an underground movement at the time. So he brought it out to the limelight when he became a Christian. He made it the religion of Rome so that it was no longer against the law to be a Christian. It was now actually honorable to be a Christian because the Emperor himself was a Christian.

What happened was that the Emperor becoming a Christian attracted a lot of pagans who came into the Christian faith, not because they liked Jesus or His message but because to be on the Emperor's side you had to be a Christian. It was the "in" thing. So when they came into the church, they came with their traditions.

That is why when you look at the Roman Catholic Madonna today, Mary went from being a peasant to a queen with a crown and lights about her head—the pagan 'Queen of Heaven!' The worship of the Sun god and the Queen of Heaven goes back to the time of Nimrod. The worship of the Sun god and the Queen of heaven was well established in Rome before Christianity came to Rome. You can read this in my book, <u>Unveiling the God-Mother</u>, because I talk extensively about these spirits.

When Nimrod died, his wife declared him to be a god (the sun god) and she declared herself as the mother of the gods—the Queen of heaven. Tradition has it that she was found to be pregnant after the death of her husband, and her brilliant explanation was that her dead husband (Nimrod) came up and mated with her at night and he also made a dead tree-stump to spring back into life and she got pregnant. That is where your Christmas tree came from because after her explanation, barren women began to bring the tree into their houses and to put ornaments on it and set up lights in their home for the sun god. They pray to the sun god to give them children and they leave a present under the tree for him. All of that came into Christianity via Constantine because when he brought the people in Rome together, everybody was like "Let's all get along" – which is what you see in the world today. Those who do not know Jesus want us to come together with them and

41

their gods so that we can all get along. They ask us evangelical Christians, "why are you guys different? You always insist on Jesus being the only way." But we know that Jesus said, I am the way, the truth and the life. No man comes to the father but by me. <u>He alone is the one we must follow</u>.

When Constantine became a Christian, he basically highjacked Christianity and made his own rules concerning it. If you look at churches today, a lot of them have steeples on them as commanded by Constantine. This steeple is actually a pagan temple! Constantine commanded that you could not build a place of worship without putting the pagan temple on top of the Christian building so that both Christians and pagans can worship together. He wanted everybody to get along. Today, you see those who are ignorant of Church history still building their churches with steeples. They do not have a clue as to what the steeple means. Also Constantine figured since the birthday of the Sun god was December 25th and Rome already celebrated it as the birthday of the god, he just included Jesus in the birthday celebration. His idea was let's just celebrate all the gods in one day.

This is why he coined the term "Christ-Mass." Mithra worshippers brought their "Mass" and Christians had "Christ." This is where we got the word "Christ-mass." So you see that **Christmas has nothing to do with the birthday of Jesus Christ. If you want to celebrate Jesus, then celebrate Jesus but leave paganism to the pagans. If somebody calls me and says I'm having a dinner in honor of the birthday of the Lord Jesus, I'll show up. But if you tell me you're celebrating Christmas, I will not show up.**

**Question #2:** *I'm Russian and we don't really celebrate Christmas in Russia. We do, but not as much as you guys do here. We celebrate New Years, New Years Eve, and we also have the Christmas tree but we don't call it Christmas tree. What would you say about it? Is it also from pagans?*

**Mary's Answer:** **I wouldn't know, but I tell you what, if it smells like a fish, it is probably a fish. Since we don't know exactly what you guys do, as I just told you, if you have a dinner and you ask me to come for the Lord's birthday, I will come. But if you have the same dinner and ask me to come for Christmas, I will not come. So you have to look into what it is that you guys are doing and analyze it to see if it Christmas in disguise or if it is something else. If it is Christmas in disguise, then don't celebrate it, but if it is only speaking to the birthday of the Lord Jesus Christ, I see nothing wrong with honoring the Lord.**

**Question #3:** *So now that we know the truth about Christmas, will we be held accountable, if we still celebrate it?*

43

**Mary's Answer:** **You are to know the truth and let the truth set you free. Whoever chooses to remain in bondage after hearing the truth has him or herself to blame.**

**Question #5:** *Since you don't celebrate Christmas as Americans do; you celebrate the birth of Christ. This is just a question, when do you think He was born? There are discrepancies about the actual birthday of Christ. Do you yourself have like a date or a round-about general time or do you just celebrate the Lord? How do you do that?*

**Mary's Answer:** **That is a very, very good question. I cannot rewrite the Bible; I cannot add to it or take out of it. We can only go by what we were told. We were not told when Jesus was born, but history will tell us that if you look at Palestine and look at the time that shepherds put out their sheep at night, we can pretty much guess that it would not be in the winter, which is the time of Christmas. It would not be in the fall, which is when shepherds take their sheep off the field. It's most likely to be in the spring; but that's just an opinion.**

**I don't think it's a matter of trying to figure the exact day or time that Jesus was born. We have to celebrate the fact that he was born and that's good enough. You should celebrate his birthday every day with your life, because people should be**

able to see Jesus in you everyday. The only way you would know that some people are Christians is because they wear a cross. Their actions are demonic but they carry the cross on their neck and it becomes a reproach to Jesus Christ. Let people see you celebrate Jesus with your life and not so much by your festivities.

# The Truth about Dreadlocks

**Question #7**: *Are you going to also touch on the subject of the dreadlocks and give us that foundation also?*

**Mary's Answer**: The subject of the dreadlocks. The dreadlock—that is a spirit. If you can see into the spirit realm, you would see that the dreadlock spirit actually looks like the spirit of poverty—the hairdo. The spirit of poverty wears fat dreadlocks and a grass skirt. That's why you see that when people begin to wear dreadlocks, the next thing that happens to them is that they begin to suffer loss in finances, in relationships and in society – people stay away from them. Dreadlocks repel any decent human being.

Just to touch on the subject of dreadlocks, where I grew up in Africa, they believe in reincarnation. They believe that there is a world of evil children who love to come into the world to torment their parents. The way they do this is that they get born into the world and they get the affection of their parents and other love ones, but when they reach a certain age they die. They are tormentors who love to be born only to die and come back again – they are on an endless journey between life and death.

The Ibos in Nigeria call these types of children 'Ogbanje' while the Yorubas call them 'Abiku'— a person born to die. The reason these children love to live briefly and then die is because they are the ringleaders in the world of evil children. Therefore at a certain age, they have an obligation to their friends in the other world to return to their ringleader position. The belief is that it is the parent's duty when a child is born to identify the one that has the dreadlocks—the one reputed to be the ringleader in the evil world! In other words, the reason you can't keep him or her here on earth is because he or she heads a clan. He or she rules over people in the other world so they need him or her back in that world after a certain time. Therefore, they can only be on earth for a brief period.

When a child is born, the parents would look to see if there is any knot on the child's hair. If they find one, they would not comb the child's hair for years. Why? Because they believe that the child would die if they comb out his or her locks. The job of the parents is to try to tie the child to this world with a bribe. They would wait until the child reaches the age of consent so that

46

they can bribe the child to accept this world and reject the evil world.

While waiting for the child to reach age of consent, the hair grows wild and the child walks about in dreadlocks until he reaches the age of 6 or 7. The belief is that when the child goes to sleep, the children in the evil world say to him or her, "You have been down there too long, come back." On the appointed day, the parents would cook and host a party in honor of the child. They would then ask the child what he or she wants in order to get the dreadlocks cut off. It was the closest thing that they had to a birthday party. The parents would spread a white cloth and set the child on a chair in the center of the white cloth.

The witch doctor would ask the child, "Are you willing to keep the friends you now have here on earth and reject the ones that are beckoning you from the evil world?" This is why they gather the child's friends on earth to come and party with the child on the appointed day. If the child says, "yes," then the next question is, "Can we cut off your ringleader locks?" (Actually dread-lock is a perversion of the anointing on Samson. Because the locks were on Samson's hair and the power was in his locks.) After they have success-fully bribed the child, because whatever the child asks for is what the parents have to give to the child in order for him or her to say yes to cutting off the locks. You see that dreadlocks speak of a child that is a ringleader of an evil world, waiting for acceptance into this world.

It really promotes the belief in reincarnation that we as Christians cannot afford to dabble in. A lot of times I see Christians with dreadlocks and when I ask them if they know what it means, they say, "it's just a hairdo." If you come across Christians wearing dreadlocks out of ignorance, hopefully, this gives you information to help them make an intelligent decision concerning their hairdo. They need to know the origin and implication of what dreadlocks means and the spirit they are embracing by wearing dreadlocks. Dreadlocks speak of reincarnation, it speaks of wickedness and we need to put these things behind us. As believers in Jesus Christ, we cannot play around with these spirits.

**Question #8:** *Does it matter the size of the locks?*

**Mary's Answer:** It doesn't matter the size of the locks; a lock is a lock.

**Question #9**: *My name is Charles and I was "born" with dreadlocks in Edo State, Nigeria. From what my parents told me, they had to perform certain ceremony to cut off the dreadlocks. It's like they had to get my permission to touch my head. They cannot cut them off without my permission. I did not grow up to see the dreadlocks. This was done when I was very young but I was told the story of the ceremony to cut* *them off. Today, I don't know the meaning and I don't know what they did to me. I am interested to find out what they did to me. What is the meaning of this? What did my parents do to me with the ceremony and who am I right now?*

**Mary's Answer:** Very good question. You see, God brought him here because he had gone through an initiation ceremony when he was so little that he didn't even know what was done to him. There are some things he has probably been battling with in life that he did not even know were the result of his having been sanctified and ordained a ring-leader of evil children by his parents at an early age. Some African parents seriously look at their children's hair when they are born to see if there are any locks. They usually don't cut them off until the child is about six years. Maybe you were too young to remember because you have to come to the age of consent before they can do anything to the hair. They don't touch you without your permission. See how sneaky the devil is? You have to give him permission to touch you. Once you go through that ceremony, then officially they think they're delivering you from being a ringleader, but what they're actually doing is handing you over to the devil—opening you up for demonic attacks.

We're going to repent of that ceremony and we're going to ask God to forgive your parents and you're going to forgive them as well. We're going to break off that initiation and set you free.

49

**I attended several of them while I was growing up because they usually provide good food. You are going to renounce whatever covenant they made on your behalf with the children that were present on that day. You are also going to renounce the ungodly friendship with the children at your initiation so that you can have good friends. You have probably been having problems with friends in your life.**

*Prayer to Remove Dreadlock Curse and Thanksgiving for Salvation*

### Mary says to Charles, "Repeat after me":
*"Father God, in the Name of Jesus, I thank you that I'm born again and that I'm Spirit-filled. I forgive my parents for putting me through the initiation ceremony—the Dada ceremony. I renounce every covenant with the Dada spirit. I declare that I'm not Dada, and I reject the dreadlocks and I say that I was not born with dreadlocks. I renounce also every confession that was spoken over me by my parents announcing that I was Dada. In the Name of the Lord Jesus Christ, I renounce the evil sanctification of my head until I got to a certain age and declare that I'm born again, Spirit-filled and a child of God. Amen.*

### Mary Prays for Charles:
*"Father, in the Name of the Lord Jesus Christ, we thank you that your son is born again. Father, we break the yoke of the covenant of Dada that was made over him at the initiation ceremony in which his head*

*was sanctified and reverenced for the first few years of his life. We break it off in Jesus' Name. We say that Jesus Christ is Lord of his life. Satan, we command you to loose him right now. You spirits of Dada, loose him and let him go. In Jesus' Name we declare that he is not a dreadlock person and that he was not born with it; therefore we cancel your assignment against. Everybody speak blessing, blessing, blessing, blessing, blessing upon him in Jesus' Name. Amen.*

# Historical Facts About the Rastafari Dreadlocks

Leonard Howell was the first to introduce the "Rastafari Theology" to Jamaicans. The rastafari theology centers on the divinity of the late Ethiopian Emperor Haile Selassie and the struggle of the black man. Rastas do not believe in Christianity and Jesus. Rastafari came out of the struggle against British colonial imperialism in Jamaica. The Rastas see themselves as the instruments of emancipation of the black race. Rastas began wearing dreadlocks as part of their rastafari ideology of the superiority of the black race and also in an attempt to instill "dread" in the hearts of their British colonial masters in Jamaica.

According to Professor Noel Leo Erskine of Emery University in his book titled, *From Garvey to Marley Rastafari Theology* (pages xiv-1), "The Bible is not the definitive source of truth for the Rastas. Their authoritative source of truth is

51

"Jah" (God) as Jah reveals Jah's ways in national or world events or in the Bible... They often begin with the sociological text and then move to the biblical text for elucidation and confirmation of what they presume Jah is doing in the world. Dread Talk became a way of lashing out against the colonial and imperial way of life in Jamaica, conditions that the Rastas referred to as "Babylon"... Dread Talk became a crucial tool of resistance in fighting the war against Babylon."

From the above historical account, we can see that dreadlocks and "Dread Talk" are not based on the principles that the Lord outlined for us as Christians. Therefore, a Christian should not ignorantly partake of the Dreadlocks and the Dread Talk of the Rastafari Movement.

# Chapter 2
# The Origin of Evil Spirits

Evil spirits, unclean spirits, devils or demons as we call them are disembodied spirits of the **Pre-Adamic beings** that lived on the earth before Lucifer rebelled against God. They joined Lucifer in his insurrection against God. As a punishment for joining in this rebellion, God stripped them of their terrestrial bodies so that they could no longer physically walk the face of the earth. In order for them to operate on earth effectively today and continue their rebellion against God, they need human bodies. They incite men to commit evil acts so they need to dwell in human bodies in order for their activities to continue.

**The Theory of Fallen Angels as Demons:**
There are many scholars that believe that evil spirits or demons are fallen angels that rebelled with Lucifer against God and were cast out of heaven with him. According to these scholars, these fallen angels are now the evil spirits or demons that now incite men to commit evil acts.

**The Theory of Nephilims as Demons:**
There are other scholars that believe that evil spirits or demons are offspring of fallen angels that mated with earthly women. In other words, fallen angels took normal, earthly women as wives and mated with them and produced giants. It is true that fallen angels mated with women and produced giants as recorded in **Genesis 6:2 and these giants lived on earth as**

53

**mighty men:**

> [2]*...The sons of God saw the daughters of men that they were fair; and they took them wives of all which they chose.*

According to this theory, when God destroyed the human race during the days of Noah, these giants became disembodied spirits. In other words, they lost their bodies when they drowned. They refer to the spirits of these giants as **"Nephilims."** Many believe that Nephilims are the spirits of the former giants that have their origin in the union of earthly woman and fallen angels. They conclude that these Nephilims are now what we call evil spirits, demons or wicked spirits.

**The problem with both of these theories about the fallen angel and the giants (the product of angels and earthly women) is that they contradict scriptures.** The scriptures prove them to be wrong. Look at **Jude 6-7**:

> [6]*And* <u>*the angels which kept not their first estate,*</u> *but left their own habitation, he (God) hath* <u>*reserved in everlasting chains under darkness unto the judgment of the great day.*</u> [7]*Even as Sodom and Gomorrha, and the cities about them in like manner, giving themselves over to fornication, and* <u>*going after strange flesh,*</u> *are set forth for an example, suffering the vengeance of eternal fire.*

Angels that did not keep their "first estate" are chained, they are not around on earth to walk about as demons or evil spirits. In other words, God chained them. He's reserved them for the great judgment day. They are going to be judged. Therefore, for somebody to say that they are now the demons roaming the earth is not true. This scripture contradicts that theory. The scripture says that they are in darkness and they are chained.

Also, **II Peter 2:4** tells us the same:

> *⁴For if God spared not the angels that sinned, but cast them down to hell, and delivered them into chains of darkness, to be reserved unto judgment.*

We see from the above scripture also that fallen angels are reserved in darkness unto judgment. Because they are in chains, they are not loose to roam the earth as demons.

Also, **I Peter 3:19**:

> *¹⁹By which also he (Jesus) went and preached unto the spirits in prison; ²⁰Which sometime were disobedient, when once the longsuffering of God waited in the days of Noah, while the ark was a preparing, wherein few, that is, eight souls were saved by water.*

**The above scriptures proved that the angels that**

**sinned are chained in darkness in hell, waiting to be judged at the judgment seat of Christ, which is the final judgment.** We also see from the scripture in **Genesis 6:2**, that the giants, or Nephilims, were part human and part angel. They lived on earth as human beings. They were just exceptionally tall and massive in their body structure. That was the only difference between them and a normal person; they were huge but they were counted as humans. Scriptures again tell us in **Genesis 6:4** that giants were human beings:

> *"There were <u>giants</u> in the earth in those days; and also after that, when the <u>sons of God ( angels) came in unto the daughters of men</u> (women), and they bare children to them, the same <u>became mighty men</u> which were of old, <u>men of renown</u>."*

As human beings, giants were subject to the judgment that came upon man in the days of Noah. They drowned in the flood. As human beings, a few of them even survived up until the time of David (Goliath and his brothers). David fought with a giant man named Goliath. He did not fight with a non-human being. Scriptures tell us in **Hebrews 9:27** that:

> *[27]...It is appointed unto men once to die, but after this the judgment.*

Now you know how to respond with the Word of the Lord to someone who gives you this different account about the origin of demons. **You should tell them that demons are not fallen angels and they are not Nephilims.** This is because Nephilims or giants were human beings. Scriptures say in **Hebrews 9:27** that it is appointed unto men once to die and after that the judgment. Therefore, Nephilims are awaiting judgment just like other human being who are dead. **Just like the fallen angels that are chained in darkness, the spirits of the giants or Nephilims as we call them, are not free to roam the earth.** Their lives ended when they died just like any other human beings.

## The Covering Cherub and His Sanctuaries:

If evil spirits are not demons or fallen angels or Nephilims, what are they? The Lord gave me a direct answer to this question while I was reading a research material about the origin of demons. In this particular material, **I was reading the article that says that the scriptures do not tell us of any other beings before Adam.** And the Lord spoke to me almost audibly **saying, "That's not true. There was a covering cherub that had the covering of a class of beings." He pointed me to Ezekiel 28.** When I looked in **Ezekiel 28**, He began to show me the activities of the covering cherub.

In **Ezekiel 28**, God is addressing a spirit (which is the devil himself) that indwelled the King of Taurus and was using the King of Taurus to express his prideful, evil ways. This chapter gives us an idea of Lucifer, his role, his assigned duties and why he fell.

We must remember that the events being described in Ezekiel 28 were events that happened before Adam was created. We as human beings never saw Lucifer the way Lucifer is being described in this scripture but there was a class of beings (the pre-Adamic beings) that saw him and these beings were not angels. These are the events that led to what is called the "pre-Adamic Flood"—the flood that took place before Adam was created. During this flood, God destroyed the earth and cast out the rebels, stripping them of their terrestrial bodies. God was so angry that he literally commanded everything on earth to stop functioning! This is why **Genesis 1:2** says, "The earth was without form and void" because God in His anger almost turned the world upside down.

> **²And the earth was without form, and void; and darkness was upon the face of the deep. And the Spirit of God moved upon the face of the waters.**

The Prophet Jeremiah was given a vision of the earth as it was during the pre-Adamic Flood in **Jeremiah 4:23-25**. This is what he saw:

> *²³I beheld the earth, and, lo, it was without form, and void; and the heavens, and they had no light. ²⁴I beheld the mountains, and, lo, they trembled, and all the hills moved lightly. ²⁵I beheld, and, lo, there was no man,*

58

*and **all the birds of the heavens were fled.***

During the flood in Noah's days, God never commanded the light to stop shining. It just rained for 40 days but during this flood, there was no light—the sun and the moon were commanded not to shine. When God first created the earth, the earth was perfect. God never creates anything that is chaotic. So it makes you wonder what happened between **Genesis 1:1** and **Genesis 1:2**.

> *¹In the beginning God created the heaven and the earth.²And the earth was without form, and void; and darkness was upon the face of the deep. And the Spirit of God moved upon the face of the waters.*

Billions of years went into those little verses because whatever God does is perfect and beautiful so it is a serious thing for what God created to become "without form and void." What we found out is that He gave a covering cherub charge over the sanctuaries on the earth and the covering cherub got prideful. So something happened. This is why **Genesis 1:3** begins with God restoring the earth back to the original condition before the pre-Adamic Flood. He was commanding things to appear that had been before and that He commanded to stop functioning when He was angry.

Now let us look at Ezekiel 28. Really try to understand this scripture because you should be able to teach it to others. When someone asks you what are demons, you should be able to explain it to them very concisely.  Let us look at **Ezekiel 28: 13-19**. I'm going to start from verse 14 because I am reserving verse 13 for later.

> *14Thou art the <u>anointed cherub that covereth</u>; and I have set thee so: thou wast upon the holy mountain of God; <u>thou hast walked up and down in the midst of the stones of fire.</u> 15<u>Thou wast perfect in</u> thy ways from the day that thou wast created, <u>till iniquity was found in thee.</u> 16By the <u>multitude of thy merchandise they have filled the midst of thee with violence,</u> and <u>thou hast sinned</u>: therefore I will cast thee as profane out of the mountain of God: <u>and I will destroy thee, O covering cherub, from the midst of the stones of fire.</u> 17Thine heart was lifted up because of thy beauty, thou hast <u>corrupted thy wisdom by reason of thy brightness:</u> I will cast thee to the ground, I will lay thee before kings, that they may behold thee. <u>18Thou hast defiled thy sanctuaries by the multitude of thine iniquities, by the iniquity of thy traffick</u>; therefore will I bring forth a fire from the midst of thee, it shall devour thee, and I will bring thee to ashes upon the earth in the sight of all them that behold thee. 19<u>All they that know thee among the people shall be astonished at thee:</u> thou shalt be a terror, and never shalt thou be any more.*

Let's highlight some key points in this scripture.

(i)    The first thing you need to know is that Lucifer was called the **covering cherub**.

(ii)   The next thing you need to know is that **he**

walked in the midst of the stones of fire—
he had experienced the power of God.

(iii)    He was **created perfect.**

(iv)    Iniquity was found in him. **Iniquity is the
tendency to do your own thing in your own
way to produce sin, the tendency to bend
towards sin.** That is why it is what is passed
on from generation to generation, because if
you watch your father do something, chances
are you're going to do what you saw him do
because he passed it on to you. It takes four
generations to break an act of iniquity from
a family. God Himself promised to visit the
iniquity of those that hate Him on their offspring even to the fourth generation!

(v)    He engaged in what the Bible calls **"the act
of merchandising"** and **it filled him with
violence.**

(vi)    He **sinned**.

(vii)    He **was prideful because of his beauty**.

(viii)    He was **also given a lot of wisdom but he
corrupted it** because he began to look to his
own brightness.

(ix)    He **defiled his sanctuaries** by the iniquity of
his trafficking.

(x)    God promised to **bring him to ashes and to
destroy him.**

Now, let's address what all the above means. To
summarize, what the scripture is saying here is that
Lucifer was anointed to cover. God does not need
a cherub to cover Him. Some people say that Lucifer was covering God but this is not true because the

lesser is covered by the greater. God is greater than Lucifer so He does not need any other being to cover Him. Lucifer was the praise and worship leader that led the worship of the Living God. What does a praise and worship leader do during worship? He brings people before the presence of the Lord. As the covering cherub, Lucifer was to bring the pre-Adamic beings before God in worship. He was also the light bearer—he had the revelation concerning God and his job was to teach these beings about God. Therefore, he was very bright (filled with wisdom) and he was given charge over "the sanctuaries of worship" on earth. In other words, he had the revelation of who God is before these beings and he was supposed to illuminate these "people" (in verse 19). Also, he was filled with a lot of wisdom because he had to be able to answer questions from these "people" when they asked about God. Therefore, everything he had was given to him in order for him to effectively bring the "sanctuaries of worship" before the Lord during praise and worship. But something happened because iniquity began to surface in Lucifer.

Now, we will look at **Ezekiel 28:13**:

> [13]*Thou hast been in Eden the garden of God; every precious stone was thy covering, the sardius, topaz, and the diamond, the beryl, the onyx, and the jasper, the sapphire, the emerald, and the carbuncle, and gold: the workmanship of thy tabrets and of thy pipes was prepared in thee in the day that thou wast created.*

God invested all these in Lucifer. Why? Because he was the praise and worship leader. He could sing and help the pre-Adamic beings rise up to worship God. He did not have to look for anything outside of himself, except be dependent on the Lord and be humble, knowing that all the things he had were given to him for service. He did not create them by himself. He was a created being and not a creator but he forgot this vital fact. When he looked at himself and saw how bright he was and all the wisdom that he had and how all the pre-Adamic beings looked to him for answers because he was God's representative or messenger to them, he became prideful. As he began to think too highly of himself, iniquity surfaced. God revealed what was in Lucifer's heart as he became prideful when iniquity surfaced in him in **Isaiah 14:13**:

> *Thou hast said in thine heart **I will ascend into heaven, I will exalt my thrones above the stars of God** (which are angels). **I will sit also in the mount of the congregation.***

I tell you again that there were a people that formed Lucifer's congregation. Because he had a congregation, he began to desire worship and he also wanted to sit on the sides of the north and in the midst of the congregation just like God!

*I will sit also in the mount of the*

63

**_congregation_** (in the midst of the pre-Adamic beings)**, *in the sides of the North. I will ascend above the heights of the clouds. I will be like the Most High.*** (This was the iniquity.)

Lucifer forgot for one minute that he was not God. Because he was able to lead these beings in praise and worship and because he was able to represent the beauty and wisdom of God before them, it went to his head and he became prideful. God looked at him and said I have a problem with you. This is why we must be humble no matter the level of anointing and gifting we are operating in because whatever we have is a gift from God. The minute you forget that it is a gift, that old pre-Adamic being named the devil knows it very well, and he will come looking for you as an ally. Iniquity was found in him and he is quick to visit those who choose iniquity. Do not be like Lucifer who forgot that the musical abilities, the beauty and wisdom that he had were all given to him for service.

I can interpret dreams; I can ask you to tell me your dream or vision and before you're done I will get the answer. Did I come up with the answer? No! The Lord gave that ability to me. I know that it is a gift from God. God the Father came into my bedroom and before He left He said: "By the way your dream means…" —that's how I got it! The minute you forget that what you have is a gift, you can fall. Lucifer was the highest ranked angel in heaven. That is why the scriptures talk about how Michael could not rebuke satan before the Lord Jesus came and took away satan's authority. All Michael could say to him was, "The Lord rebuke thee satan." The reason was because satan was higher in authority and position than Michael. But despite all that God gave satan, he was not satisfied and he wanted to take the worship that the pre-Adamic beings were giving to God for himself. Let us look at how sad it is for one to be given so much and yet be so greedy. Before we look at the activities of Lucifer again, I want to remind you that **when God created the earth, He created it for habitation. He never created it in vain.** We read this in <u>Isaiah 45:18</u>:

> *[18]For thus saith the LORD that created the heavens; God himself that formed the earth and made it; he hath established it, <u>he created it not in vain, he formed it to be inhabited</u>: I am the LORD; and there is none else.*

When God created the earth, He created it for a class of beings to inhabit. He always wanted somebody to live on this earth because that is how He likes it. It is the whole purpose of why He created the earth—for habitation. He desired to dwell with people on earth.

Now, let us go back and look at Lucifer some more. As a result of the beauty, the gifts and everything else that he had, he began to corrupt his wisdom and to traffick in iniquity. Remember, the Bible says in Ezekiel 28:18, **"<u>Thou hast defiled thy sanctu-</u>**

65

**aries by the multitude of thine iniquities, by the iniquity of thy traffick...**" To traffick in something means to have a commercial exchange: to engage in illegal or improper commercial activity. We know that Lucifer was not into buying and selling of physical goods. **What he was merchandising to these pre-Adamic beings that formed the congregation, was himself as their God in place of the Living God.** He began to teach these beings to look to him instead of God. That's why the spirit of blasphemy or profanity is one of the first spirits to attack you when you truly get born again and get filled with the Holy Spirit. The devil sends difficult situations against you because he wants you to blaspheme God for allowing the difficult situations to come your way. He wants you to speak against God or against the things of God when the things he sends your way press you heavily. He will send people your way with conversations aimed at defiling your tongue. He began to teach the pre-Adamic beings blasphemy and rebellion against God. Unfortunately for these pre-Adamic beings that formed the congregation and sanctuaries that Lucifer was in charge of, they cast in their lots with him and rebelled against God. **He defiled them!**

This is why God said to him in **Ezekiel 28:18**:

> *[18]Thou **hast defiled thy sanctuaries** by the multitude of thine iniquities, **by the iniquity of thy traffick;***

When we look at the word "**sanctuary,**" we get an even clearer idea of Lucifer's former role on earth.

*A sanctuary is a sacred place of worship, like a church or a temple. It is also a place of refuge or protection for animals or beings. A sanctuary cannot exist where you have no beings.* **So you see that there were pre-Adamic beings that made up the sanctuaries and congregation to whom Lucifer was merchandising iniquities and trafficking iniquity.** Unfortunately for these beings they bought into Lucifer's rebellion against God.

Lucifer was actually in charge of the sanctuaries over the earth; there evidently were many of them all over the earth that constituted the places of worship of God. When he had successfully defiled these beings and corrupted them, he convinced them to march with him into heaven so that he could set up his own throne so that praise and worship could ascend to him also. Whoever he was going to use as his praise and worship leader is still out there! He also convinced a third of the angels to join in this rebellion. God, in anger, cast him and his angels down to the earth and flooded the earth. Lucifer, the rebellious angels and the pre-Adamic beings were stripped of their terrestrial bodies. This is why they can no longer walk up and down the earth in the physical form. God chained the angels in darkness to keep them from corrupting the Adamic race that replaced the pre-Adamic beings. Demons are angry with us because we replaced them and it is the reason why they want to make the fate of human beings as theirs. Because they are now doomed to be destroyed, they want to take many people with them to hell. Hell was built for the devil, fallen angels and demons. It was never built for man. It is demons that incite men to commit evil acts and the evil acts lead human beings to hell.

Both the devil formerly known as Lucifer and the pre-Adamic beings are not chained in darkness. Only the angels that sinned are chained. There is a reason – the devil has been judged, because Jesus tells us in **John 16:11** that the prince of this world has been judged.

> *11Of judgment, because the prince of this world is judged.*

The devil has been judged. **The pre-Adamic beings will be judged by the new creation—the new man, which is us!** This is why the legions of evil spirits in the demoniac said, **"have you come to destroy us before the time?"** There is a set time for their destruction. From this we see that God has set an appointed time for the pre-Adamic beings, now evil spirits to be judged. We the children of God in Christ Jesus must first learn obedience, because it will be our duty to judge these beings after we have demonstrated our obedience to God. **Meanwhile, we the church, the Children of God, have to demonstrate to these evil spirits—the pre-Adamic beings that it is possible to obey God and resist the devil.** We are to demonstrate the manifold wisdom of God to them and angels.

We are to contend with them because we are to punish them for willingly siding with the devil. **We are a living testimony that you can**

**resist the devil and obey God.** And when we have successfully done this as the Church of Jesus Christ, the next thing is to judge the pre-Adamic beings because they sinned; they could have resisted the devil and looked unto God.

# Questions and Answers

Question #1: *Do you believe a person can have a demon that cannot be cast out without the coopera- tion of the person's own will? I have come across situations in my experience where some people seem to be so attached to a spirit, (bad attitude, depres- sion, anguish, sex, cigarette smoking, etc.) that they don't want to be delivered from it. If they don't want a release, can a Christian expel the demon anyway?*

*Mary's Answer:* **The one thing that God never tempers with in a man is the will. He never overrides a person's will. He told me once that a person has the right to go to hell if that is what the person wills. A person has to willingly surrender his or her will. Therefore, if a person does not want you to pray for them or cast out any spirit from them, you leave the person alone. Even the Lord Jesus always asked, "What do you will that I do for you?" He did this to in order to respect the people's will. A lot of Christians open themselves up for demonic attacks by overriding people's will and praying or casting out spirits from people without the people's consent. Some have even died as a result of this. There are people going around**

69

today binding other people to the will of God or to the Word of God. This is witchcraft prayer and it needs to stop. God respects a person's will and we must do the same also. Each person alive must choose life or death. No one can make the choice for them once they reach the age of consent.

I usually take authority over any spirit that rises up against me in a person but I never go into casting out spirit from a person without the person's consent. Parents on the other hand, have legal authority to cast out a spirit from their child or give permission for a spirit to be cast out of their child because they have legal authority over their children.

**Question #2:** *I do in fact teach and practice that there are several ways of taking authority over devils. I wandered if you teach certain techniques in your class.*

**_Mary's Answer:_** Yes, I am going to teach on that in Chapter 6 of this book that deals with <u>How To Expel Evil Spirits</u>. There are several ways to cast out a spirit without making a scene.

**Question #3:** *Would you think there are certain settings where calling out a demon is not appropriate (Such as in a restaurant, a bank or a library)? Or do you talk of some specific ways to cast out devils other than screaming out, " <u>YOU COME OUT OF HIM, UNCLEAN SPIRIT?</u> "*

*Mary's Answer:* **When I am in a public place, I do not have to act crazy like the devil by commanding out loud, "come out...." The Lord taught me the power of the name of Jesus. When a spirit confronts me in a public place, I look at the spirit in the eye squarely and declare, "Jesus is Lord." The spirit will immediately bow or run when it hears the name of Jesus. There are times when I am meeting a person for the first time and the evil spirit in them begins to manifest or register its presence. I just say, Jesus is Lord and the person will even agree with me and the spirit in them will flee.**

*Question #4: Was it the angel Michael that cast the devil out?*

*Mary's Answer:* **The Bible doesn't actually say who it was exactly that cast him out, but from what I deduced in the scriptures, God said, "I will cast you to the ground, remember?" So, I would say that God did it. Michael contends with him because Michael is also an archangel. But now the devil is so low that even the least angel is higher than him.**

*Question #5: Are you saying the angels walked on earth and that they had human terrestrial bodies before they were cast out?*

*Mary's Answer:* **You want to know if the angels were once terrestrial? Do you know that the good**

71

angels can still walk about the earth and appear
to you as me if they so choose?  They can appear
to you as a human being.  That is how all angels
used to be but then the angels that sinned had
to be chained so that they can no longer come
and deceive women.  Before they were chained,
they could go and represent themselves to you as
your husband when your husband is away.  An
angel could show up at your house and you'd be
thinking it's your husband and engage in sexual
acts with him.  They have supernatural abilities to
flow between earth and heaven.  They could come
and present themselves to women and deceive the
women.  God didn't want that on our shoulders,
so for our sake (the Adamic race), he chained them.
But the evil spirits we are to punish.

***Question #6:***   *Can you elaborate on the four
generational curses?*

***Mary's Answer:***   It takes four generations to
overcome an act of iniquity.  The reason being for
example, if she was my daughter and I told her
something, she's going to tell it to her daughter a
little bit different from the way I told it to her and
her daughter is going to tell it to her daughter in a
little different way also.  By the time it gets to the
fourth generation, it is not faithful to what I said
originally.  The iniquity that was passed on is not
faithfully passed beyond the fourth generation.
It's just like passing a message from one person to
another and to another.  By the time you get to the

72

fifth person, your message is distorted. That's why, in most cases, iniquities are broken by the fourth generation because people add things to them as they pass them on to the next generation. By the fourth generation, it doesn't appear anything like the original iniquity.

*Question #7: I'm not sure the answer is recorded anywhere in the Bible, but I was just curious since angels and demons were created or whatever, have they multiplied or are they the same number as before? I don't know if that's in the Bible anywhere.*

*Mary's Answer:* Do you remember that only Adam was ever told by God to "Be fruitful and multiple?" We as human beings came from Adam and therefore can multiply. Angels do not have the ability to procreate. What did Jesus say? He said, by the end you'll be "like angels who neither marry nor are given in marriage."

*Question #8: I have a question concerning the number of demons that are here today. I was under the impression that demons were towards the end-time because it clearly states in the Bible that time will come when men will get wicked and wicked and also in Jeremiah God says He pull out His weapons and His armory for the end-time. So there are new weapons we must use to annihilate evil. So I'm assuming there's more demons released out of hell during the end-time?*

**Mary's Answer:** You always have to remember what the scriptures say about when man is enticed and when man lust after something. Lust does what when it conceives? It brings forth sin and sin when it conceives brings forth death. Eve lusted after the forbidden fruit and she gave Adam the fruit to eat also. Therefore when Adam ate the fruit, he willingly submitted himself to the devil and him and his descendants became servants to the devil. Demons also did the same; they willingly submitted themselves to the devil and became his servants. Therefore, they're directly under his control. What he does is, he sends them out as the demand for wickedness increases on earth because demons help people accomplish or facilitate evil desires. They will first of all plant the idea in a person and then they will work on the person and help the person until the person actually commit the sin. The devil and his demons would sell a person their evil ideas because that is what they do. The devil's job is to "traffick iniquity" to people. He trafficks ideas, he trafficks blasphemy, he trafficks stuff but our job is to reject his evil ideas. This is why when a person commits an evil act, the devil can declare that he didn't make the person do anything and claim that he only just presented an idea to the person but the choice was the person's to say yes or no. This is what a trafficker does; he's slick.

Demons are released as the demand for them through lustful desires increases. If somebody is sitting on their bed and planning how he or she is going to buy an "uzzi" to spray some place, know that there's a demon behind the idea. The demon would then call other demons and say to them, " we have a buyer here and we have the merchandise." The next thing you know, the person becomes very brilliant at plotting the evil act. The demons begin to give the person "wisdom" on how to go about getting the evil act accomplished; but one thing they never prepare the person for is what to do when he or she gets caught! They can't protect the person but they will inspire the person and show the person all the evil things that the person can do and how the person can accomplish them. As soon as the person commits the act of wickedness, they would all go to the "next victim!"

# Chapter 3
# Activities of Evil Spirits

Now that we know about the origin of demons and their nature, we need to find out what they do and how they do what they do. Demons are the devil's tools for working destruction, demotion, shame, reproach, sickness, diseases and premature death in the life of people. For example, there is a class of evil spirits that are called "familiar spirits." They are spirits that are sent by the devil to do his bidding. Always remember that the pre-Adamic beings willingly yielded themselves to the devil and as result, he is now their lord. He tells them what to do. They have become totally enslaved by him and they have totally taken on the nature of the devil. He sends them into families to monitor the members and to carry out his evil intentions against the family. This is why the root word is **"familidris"** or **"familia"** which in Latin means family. They are sent into a particular family to operate in that family alone.

When familiar spirits come into a family they monitor the habits, they monitor the dislikes and they monitor the life of the members of the family. Why? Because they have to effectively "misrepresent" you to somebody in a vision or a dream. This is why you sometimes hear someone saying that somebody that had died in his or her family came back to him or her in a vision or in a dream and they're talking to the dead person. Some familiar spirits even give such people counsel in visions and dreams. When you see your dead relative in a vision or dream, know that you are dealing with a familiar spirit that monitored the habits of that dead relative and knows how that relative operated in his or her lifetime and now wants to portray that relative to you. Why? Because they lost their home (the body of that dead relative) and so the spirits are now looking for the next person who will welcome them into their body. The devil knows that if he shows you his face in a vision or dream, you are not going to welcome him into your life. But, if he comes with a face you know (a dead relative), he can beguile you and come into your life. This is why familiar spirits are very dangerous.

They come to you with the faces of people you know; people you had relationship with because they want you to welcome them into your life. If you know that the faces you see in your visions or dreams are of people that are dead, that is a clue that you need to shut the door on familiar spirits right away and not allow them to come into your life. Basically, their goal is to come into a family and convince members of that family that certain sicknesses and diseases run in their family. This is why some people can easily tell you that hypertension, diabetes, premature death, etc. run in their family. They have become a mouth-piece for these familiar spirits and they help the devil perpetuate afflictions on their family members without any hope of anybody getting delivered. They speak the devil's words over their family instead of speaking God's Word over their family. God Word says in **Isaiah 54:17** that:

> _17No weapon that is formed against thee shall prosper; and every tongue that shall rise against thee in judgment thou shalt condemn. This is the heritage of the servants of the LORD, and their righteousness is of me, saith the LORD._

This means that if someone comes to you, be it a member of your family and tells you that this and that run in your family, you should stop the person right there and say, "not in my family because I'm born again now. My heritage is now in Christ Jesus and nothing evil runs in it." You should stop that person right then because if you don't, those familiar spirits will stay and work evil in each generation and when that generation is successfully destroyed, they will check into the next one. They cannot go to another family because their assignment is specific to a particular family. Be careful about familiar spirits because they will follow you and monitor your actions if you allow them.

One thing you have to know about familiar spirits is that they also respond to your lust. The devil cannot operate where there is no rebellion or some kind of inner lust: lust of life, lust for sex, lust after money, pride, etc. He looks for those things because those things give way for familiar spirits to come into a person's life. This is why **James 1:14** says:

*14But every man is tempted, when he is drawn away of his own lust, and enticed.15Then when lust hath conceived, it bringeth forth sin: and sin, when it is finished, bringeth forth death.*

The job of familiar spirits is to place something before you, if they know that you like something lustful, maybe fornication, stealing, pedophilia etc., they make sure that you see it and they highlight to you the opportunity to do it. They will keep working on you until you actually of your own free will choose to commit the act. The minute you choose to commit the act, they will begin to give you more inspiration and when you commit the act, they then back away. This is why familiar spirits are dangerous because they will incite you to commit an evil act and back away and watch you fall. They would then turn around and mock and condemn you for having been so stupid. That is why when you see a person that has committed a horrible act finally apprehended, this "formerly bad and dangerous person" now looks like a little washed up rat. Why? Because those evil spirits that incited the person to commit the sin have checked out. They've gone on to another person.

Evil spirits incite people to commit acts of adultery, blasphemy against God (they especially love to blaspheme God). The Lord told me personally that the reason the devil wars with us in our mind is because when Jesus went into Hell to tread on the devil, one of the things He did before He took the key away from the devil was yanked the devil's tongue out. That's why he fights you in the mind. He cannot speak to you directly so he is looking for people who will speak for him. You have to be careful not to let him use your tongue because he has none of his own. He loves profanity, brutality, covetousness, depression, envy, evolution, evil force, false religion, fear, doubt, unbelief homosexuality, idolatry, infidelity, greed, intimidation, jealousy, lying, cheating – you name it. The devil loves it when he incites people to do all these things and they obey him. Evil spirits cannot operate successfully on earth without a human body. This is something you always have to remember and it is why the scripture in **Romans 12:1** tells us to present our bodies a living sacrifice unto God.

> *[1]I beseech you therefore, brethren, by the mercies of God, that ye present your bodies a living sacrifice, holy, acceptable unto God, which is your reasonable service.*

If you are conscious of this, then your body does not become something the devil can use as his own tool because it becomes a vessel sanctified for God's use only and not for any unclean spirits.

In **Matthew 12:43-45**, Jesus tells us about the desperation of evil spirits when it comes to a human body. He tells us that when an unclean spirit is cast out and the person leaves him or herself void, in other words, the person does not fill him or herself up with the Word of the Lord, it is like a clean house that is empty and I also say to you that when the devil comes to a person and sees that there is no Word of

God in the person to challenge him, he gets very happy. If he sees no Word of God in a person that has been delivered from his previous wickedness against the person, he feels the person is a safe place for him to come back to— it is a really clean house now for him to really spread out his evil roots. One of things the devil fears is the Word of God.

> *⁴³When the unclean spirit is gone out of a man, he walketh through dry places, seeking rest, and findeth none. ⁴⁴Then he saith, I will return into my house from whence I came out; and when he is come, he findeth it empty, swept, and garnished. ⁴⁵Then goeth he, and taketh with himself seven other spirits more wicked than himself, and they enter in and dwell there: and the last state of that man is worse than the first. Even so shall it be also unto this wicked generation.*

There is a networking of evil spirits—they help each other out. For instance, when a person is suffering attacks from the spirit of suicide, you say the person is suicidal. Well, the spirit of suicide is not the first spirit to attack that person. First, the spirit of discouragement comes— it tells the person how everything is not going the person's way, how nobody loves the person and it ushers in the spirit of depression. These two spirits will work on the person for a while. When the person is successfully depressed and feels like nothing is going his or her way, then the spirit of suicide comes and says, "You know, now is really the time to end it all." There might even be several other spirits that will jointly work on a person before the spirit of suicide comes in for the kill. If you have the gift to look into the realm of the Spirit, sometimes you will see that some spirits piggyback on other spirits in order to afflict one person. Sometimes when you are dealing with a person who is manifesting a particular affliction, also watch out for the other spirit that laid the network for the primary spirit to come in for the kill.

This is why after a person is delivered from an unclean spirit, the person needs to fill him or herself up with the Word of the Lord because you do not want to be an empty house void of the Word of the Lord. If the devil sees ignorance in you or sees that you do not even know what you have been delivered from, then he feels like he can come back – he can come back into you and re-enter you. I once went to a place and the Lord told me "Don't pray in this place because if you do the state of this family will be worse than before you came. Don't stir up something and leave because the spirits will flee at the Name of Jesus because they have to. But because they have legal grounds, they can come back very angry." I then noticed that they had so many doors open to the devil in their home and that they ignorantly have personal invitations left and right for the devil to come through the items in their home.

# Ways Evil Spirits Enter Into People

**Personal and Ancestral Sins:** Acts of sins are actually a direct invitation for the devil or evil spirits to come into a family, a person or a place. Your sins and the sins of the generations before you can open a door for evil spirits in your life, your family, your dwelling places, or any other thing you possess. They usually result in what we call "generational curses," because these curses are passed on from one generation to another. This is because acts of iniquities are passed on from one generation to another. **"Iniquity" is the tendency to bend or lean towards evil or evil acts**. If you watch your father or your mother do something, chances are you are going to do it. Sometimes you would hear men who watched their father abuse their mother say, "I will never do that!" Then they get married and subconsciously they start doing the same thing because the iniquity was passed on to them. The men would then have children and their children would watch them and they in turn would do the same thing. As I stated before, it usually takes about four generations to overcome the habit of iniquity. When you willfully commit an act of sin, you are really inviting evil spirits into your life. Their job is to help facilitate acts of sin.

I had a question from someone that stated that the evil spirit kept tormenting King Saul and that David would go and play godly music and the spirit would depart from Saul, but when David would leave, the spirit would come back again to torment Saul. The question was, "Was it the rebellious nature of King Saul that caused the evil spirit to keep coming back?" I replied, "No, Saul picked up that spirit when he went to consult a witch—it was a result of Saul's personal sin in consulting a witch!" Remember that Saul went to a witch to help him call up the soul of the late Prophet Samuel? **When he started dabbling in <u>necromancy</u> (consulting the dead) and began to call up the spirit of the dead, he made a covenant with the evil spirit so it followed him. As long as that covenant was in place, that spirit had a right to afflict him** but it would flee whenever he received godly ministry from David. When the atmosphere went back to what it was before David's ministry, the evil spirit would come back.

Acts of sin open a person up to attacks of evil spirits. There is no remission of sin without repentance and only the blood of Jesus can wash away sins. The scriptures did not tell us that Saul repented of his sins.

**Idolatry:** Idolatry—the worship of satan opens a person up for demonic attacks. It is how the demons themselves got into trouble with God because they willingly agreed to worship the devil instead of worshipping the Living God. As a result, they are experts in inciting men to commit idolatry because they know that it is one way that you can easily fall from grace. Speaking of idolatry and those who choose to worship idols, God said in **Isaiah 41:24:**

> *[24]Behold, ye are of nothing, and your work of nought: <u>an abomination is he that chooseth you.</u>*

If you really want God to reject you and drop you like a hot potato, begin to worship something other than the Living God. This is why when you look at the Old Testament, you will notice that on several occasions, God was furious with the children of Israel and it was usually over worshipping other gods. They were worshipping idols. God gave them over to their enemies and allowed them to be carried away captive because of idolatry. God hates idolatry. Anybody that engages in idolatry opens him or herself up for demonic attacks and the person becomes abominable to God. The devils will just check into that person's life and into the person's dwelling place and begin to work evil.

We are to worship God through His Son Jesus Christ. God commands every knee to bow "at the Name of Jesus." This is recorded in **Philippians 2:10-11**:

*[10]That at the name of Jesus every knee should bow, of things in heaven, and things in earth, and things under the earth; [11]And that every tongue should confess that Jesus Christ is Lord, to the glory of God the Father.*

I say again that, God commanded every living being to bow at the Name of Jesus. In other words, do not bow to anything less. This is why when Jesus confronted the devil, **He said, 'It is written, thou shall worship the Lord thy God, Him only shall you serve.** This is also what we are to say to any unclean spirit that tries to inspire us to worship them or other things. If the devil comes and tells you to worship him, you are to tell him off with the Word of God. When you have no real time for God and are caught up in your job, in your children, in whatever you are doing, they become the idol in your life. They become the things that drive you and before you know it, the devil comes in and builds a stronghold in your life with it. We need to find way to love the things we love and not make an idol out of them because if you do you are opening yourself up for demonic invasion.

Sometimes a spouse will make the other spouse an idol in his or her life. One danger in doing this is that you set up your spouse to be torn down by God because whatever idol you set up, God visits. There is a day of judgment for any idol you set up. So if you set your spouse as an idol or whatever you set up, you are just setting them up to be judged by God, and God is going to bring them to nothing before you just to let you know that your spouse is just another human being existing only by His grace. This is why I do not let anybody set me up as their idol and I try not to set up anybody as my idol because if I do, there is judgment both ways.

**Involvement in Occult:** If you know people who are involved in the occult and you also know that there is occult in your background, quickly repent of that because involvement in the occult opens families and whole generations and future generations to evil spirits and their activities. For instance, when a person gets initiated into Freemasonry, one of the initiation rites is to drag the "initiate" (the person

87

being initiated) with a noose on his neck into the place of initiation and "slap" the initiate in the face and the initiate falls to the ground. When the initiate gets up, he confesses that, "It is no longer him that lives but "Hiram Abiff" (the devil himself) that now lives in him." Just as we Christians say, "It is no longer I that lives but Christ that lives in me." Their confession is the opposite of the Christian confession. As a result of this evil confession, both him and whatever seed (future offspring) he carries in him when he made the evil confession or pledged, automatically become the property of the evil spirit called Hiram Abiff. Hiram Abiff is the spirit that is at the head of Freemasonry. Therefore, the spirit of Hiram Abiff has the legal right to afflict him and all his generations after him. This is why when someone discovers that their ancestors were or are involved in Freemasonry the person needs to repent immediately for their entire family because initiation into the Freemasonry is a total sanctification (dedication) of the person to evil spirits. The devil has a legal right to the person and the person's children.

**False Religion:** Another way evil spirits get into people is through false religion. False doctrines and false religions are the devil's tools to come into people's lives because once you fall into that which is not of God, you are really opening yourself up to the devil to teach and inspire you. Examples of this are the terrorists groups. Their devil-given zeal leads them to blow up other people as well as themselves in the name of a god that rewards wickedness. False doctrines have blinded them to the truth that the One

True God is a good God. He rewards the good and punishes the wicked. This is why we must stay away from false doctrines and false religion such as Islam, Buddhism, Hinduism, Eckankar, Bahai, etc.

**Evil Covenants:** Another way that evil spirits will come into a person is through evil covenants. Be careful who you make covenants with. Even handshakes that you make – if you do not believe in what a person is saying, do not agree with them in a handshake. Do not say, "Oh yes, I hear you and I agree" and shake their hand. A handshake is consent. The Lord told me, "You cannot cast out any spirit that you have extended an arm of fellowship to." Renounce all ungodly handshakes and deals. When I meet people and before I extend my hand and come into agreement with a handshake, I first make sure that I know what I am coming into agreement with. If you make a covenant or deal with a handshake and it results in affliction in your life, you can fast and pray and wonder why you are not able to gain victory over a particular spirit. If you do not know that it as a result of your handshake, you can suffer affliction all your life because a handshake is a valid covenant. Again, a very good example was the spirit that tormented King Saul in the Old Testament. Saul had a covenant with the spirit and until Saul repents and renounces that covenant, the evil spirit had the right to afflict him whenever there was no godly music playing around his house. Also, Adam is another good example. Every single person who is not born again is under the covenant Adam made with the devil. God cannot move until a person

89

chooses to come out of the Adamic covenant with the devil and come into the new covenant with the Lord Jesus. This is why salvation is of your free will – it is not something anyone can do for you, you have to choose the new covenant established by the blood of Jesus and renounce the old covenant that Adam made with the devil on your behalf.

**Evil Desires:** If you desire lustful things, the devil is out there to help you accomplish it. Therefore, be careful what you desire because you might be inviting evil spirits against your love ones and yourself. This is why God said to Cain in **Genesis 4:7:**

> 7 *If thou doest well, shalt thou not be accepted?* **and if thou doest not well, <u>sin lieth at the door. And unto thee shall be his desire,</u> and thou shalt rule over him.**

We know from scripture that Cain's desire was to commit sin and that he yielded to sin, which was already waiting for him at the door, and he killed his brother Abel. Again, I say to you that the devil releases evil spirits to help people fulfill their evil desires. They give people evil inspirations on how to accomplish evil acts. Always bring your desires into subjection to the Word of God.

**Evil or Violent Act:** Acts such as incest, rape, murder, homosexuality, promiscuity, and prostitution and evil physical attacks can bring evil spirits into somebody. These acts involve transference of spirits. For example, when a person with an evil spirit rapes a woman, it is not enough for the woman to be treated by a doctor, she needs to be cleansed of the spirit which made the man commit the act against her so that she too will not give birth to a rapist because she now carries the spirit and can to pass it on to the generations after her. That is also why when you look at some families, you find that somebody killed someone and then another person killed someone, and it continues on and on. There is always someone being killed in each generation because nobody has taken authority over the spirit to renounce the covenant or repent of the act of violence that was committed so that the whole family can be set free.

When you look at your family and you see some patterns, look to see if the patterns are covenants; if there is a pattern of generational poverty, promiscuity, etc. For example, there was a lady that was sharing something with me about her personal life and relationship and I asked her, "Did your dad marry your mom?" According to her, her mother had her and her sisters out of wedlock and nobody in several generations that she could remember among the women had been married. They were just having babies without the marriage covenant. I told her, "You need to ask the Lord to help you find out what happened." One of the reasons she needs to do this is because, sometimes we can find out that somebody jilted someone (a fiancée) in a very horrible way and brought a curse on him or her and the generations to come. Therefore, you find such people and their children unable to get married because they did something horrible concerning marriage to another person. You have to repent of this sin so that the door can be opened in your life for you to move on with a blessing instead of a curse.

**Evil Objects:** Evil things people bring into their homes can open their home up for evil spirits. A very good example of this is my visitation to a house with a lady minister from Mexico. She was visiting from Mexico and I thought she was rather interesting because she lives in a very rough part of Mexico and she had a permit to carry a gun. She was the first minister that I knew who was "armed and dangerous" physically. She had wanted to meet me because she liked my intercessory gifts. I met with her and another lady joined us and said, "I want you guys to come to my house and pray over my house." Well, she lived in a very, very expense house and neighborhood and their house was probably worth $1 million. We went and it was so funny because as I was about to cross the threshold into the house, the Holy Spirit said to me, "You are not to pray in this house." I said, 'OK'. So we went into the house and she gave us a tour of the house. She showed us some very expensive paintings. According to her, her husband purchased them in Asia and I could see that a very demonically inspired artist had painted them. As I started looking around, I saw in their dining area, a painting of the angel of death and it looked ready to leap out through the painting because the artist really gave it an aggressive expression. Then in the living room area, over the fireplace, was a tomb and in the tomb was a woman (death). If you are spiritually sensitive, you cannot sit in the living room and not get the chills. When it was time to pray, I told them the Lord told me not to pray. They both went on and prayed and I stepped away and looked at some more paintings. I was just amazed at how someone could find things that are spiritually bad and this man had a knack for finding them.

When we came out I said to her, "Now I know why the Lord did not want me to pray in your house because you have given expression to death in your house and if I had prayed, I would have stirred them up!" She said to me, "Oh my husband would be very upset if I try to do anything to those paintings." I said, "Well God knew and I believe that it is the reason why He told me not to pray." I left well enough alone. It was not quite six months afterwards that I found out that she had become suicidal. She went into this phase of just being demonically inspired to take her own life. Finally, they got divorced and had to sell the house and I told her, "Please do not take any of those paintings, let him keep his stuff!" Some people are the cause of their own problems. The paintings were very expensive but they were demonically inspired. Do not bring things that have been used or sanctified to the worship of the devil or that draw familiar spirits or unclean spirits or devils into your house because they will open you and your home up for demonic attacks.

# Questions and Answers

***Question #1:*** *Do you have to know the particular act that took place that invited the devil? What if it was 500 years ago or something?*

***Mary's Answer:*** **There is no way you can know by yourself the particular act that took place. One thing you do have is the Holy Ghost. The Bible says that, "You have 'an unction' (the Holy Ghost) from the Holy one and you know all things." That means that the Holy Ghost will teach you all things just as Jesus told us in the book of John. What I normally do when I'm battling a spirit and the spirit puts up a resistance, I would ask the Lord for the root cause or the open door. For instance, I had a difficult time after I willingly gave up a job in New York because I wanted to do things for God and I went through a period of really hard times. When the Lord finally convicted me to get back into the job market, I wanted to get back into the job market but nobody would hire me. I have a Masters Degree and was wondering what was going on. I would go and put in an application and they would offer me a very low position job. I went into praying and fasting and I said to the Lord, "I want to know the Genesis (the beginning or origin) of this problem." As I was fasting and praying, God showed me the spirit behind my problem. It was a familiar spirit in the form of my grandfather. He was sitting down on a chair just relaxing and shaking his legs and was not bothered by my fasting and praying. It was as if**

he was saying to me, "You're no threat to me." It was relaxed and shaking his legs in comfort. It mimicked my grandfather who shook his legs a lot when he was alive. I said to God, "What is the problem, I'm doing this fasting and praying and have not eaten or drank anything for three days and the spirit is sitting pretty and shaking away its legs in comfort. What is this thing?" And He said, "Because he knows you do not know the covenant he has in place against you." I said, "What is the covenant?" I was shocked when the Lord said to me, "Remember when you heard the story that your grandfather had put a curse on your dad you said it serves him right because you were angry with your dad at the time? You took sides and became a partaker of their sin."

My dad was a young aspiring cop and one day his father paid him a surprise visit while he was on duty. He dared to ask his dad why his dad did not notify him that he was coming to visit him and his dad got angry and left. Here in America, you have to call before you visit a person, but in Africa you do not have to call and it is a 'no, no' for you to say to somebody, "You did not tell me that you were coming to visit or how long are you going to stay?" So when my dad saw his dad during this visit, he had been so influenced by the western culture that he disrespected his dad by asking the question. To my grandfather, that was an unpardonable sin. Some months later, my dad went to visit his parents in the village and bought a pair of trousers for his dad, but my grandfather was so angry that he put a curse on the trousers (he had both legs of the trousers sealed as a sign of what he had done to my dad's life) and he went and buried the trousers. He told my dad that what he did to the trousers (having the trousers legs sewn shut and buried) is what he had done to his life and my dad did not take him serious until he lost his job shortly after. My dad began to suffer hardship in the area of employment. He eventually became a government contractor in his latter years. When I was growing up, I remembered my dad and my grandmother asking my grandfather to revoke the curse and my grandfather told them that the day they produced the trousers would be the day he revokes the curse. This was years later and the trousers had rotted away in wherever place my grandfather had buried it. Both my grandfather and my dad died without the curse being revoked.

I asked the Lord what to do and He said, "Well, you partook of that sin, you took sides and you opened the door for that spirit against you. You need to repent for your dad's disrespect of his dad and for the drastic reaction of your grandfather. Forgive them both and ask me to forgive you and I will drive away that spirit." As I opened my mouth in repentance and before I was done repenting for my grandfather, I saw the familiar spirit as he got up in anger and was gone! There was no way I could have known what was behind my inability to get a good job had it not been for the Lord. What makes this story even more interesting is that three days after my repentance, I saw the Holy Ghost and do you know what He was doing? He had the trousers on his shoulder and it was as if He had gone into the woods, found the place where my grandfather had buried the trousers, dug it up and placed it on His shoulder and was carrying it away just as Jesus said, 'I've carried away your sins.' I said, "Thank you Lord" when I saw it because there was no way I would have known what I was up against.

I also had to break my mother's desire for me to work as a Administrative Assistant in the company were she was working while I was in high school. The Lord removed the "ancient typewriter" from my life when I forgave my mother for the soulish born desire that she spoke over me concerning employment in the place where she was working. Whenever you find that you have fasted and prayed and you are not getting the victory over a particular spirit, know that you are most likely dealing with a spirit operating against you through an evil covenant. You need to ask the Lord to reveal to you the covenant that is keeping the spiritual oppression in place so you can repent of it. Ask the Lord to reveal the Genesis of situations to you and you will be surprised what the Holy Ghost will show you.

*Question #2:* *When you talked about evil spirits coming into your home and being opened to that, what other ways, I mean you talked about pictures and sometimes pictures can be very obvious, but are there other things you need to be careful of, things like wind chimes, statues or those kinds of things?*

*Mary's Answer:* Yes. People who keep porcelain angels in their homes open their homes up for demonic invasion. Little angles, porcelain or figurines—they look pretty in the physical but they are traps spiritually. They open your home to demonic attack big time. I never knew this until my spiritual encounter with them. Some years ago, I used to go out with a group of evangelist to witness in Chamblee, GA, every Saturday. The year before I had my first encounter with a porcelain angel, I had led a lady and her daughter to the Lord on the street. She then took my partners and me to her home because she had a teenage son that she wanted us to lead to the Lord. We got to the house and we prayed with him and he received the Lord. I remember asking him if they had a Bible in the house and he went and got it. I told him to study the book of John so that when we came back again, he would tell me what he had learned. It was about a year afterward when we went back and as we were going back to the house, I began to smell this foul smell. I asked the Lord, "What is this smell?" He did not answer. We had to go knock on the front door. When we knocked on this lady's front door, the minute she

98

saw us, she began to cry. She said, "It's got to be God that brought you people. It's got to be God." And I said, "What is going on?" She said her son ran away and her husband left her. We asked her what happened and she said her son was causing problems in the home by being rebellious and the husband blamed her and then one thing led to another and her son ran away. Her husband moved out as soon as their son ran away so she lost both her husband and her son. As she spoke, I began to smell a really foul spirit in the house. I always plead the Blood of Jesus before I enter into any home and I also declare the Lordship of Jesus. The lady then asked us to pray that God will give her victory – she wanted her husband and her son back. The most amazing thing happened when we all held hands to pray. Believe it or not when we held hands to pray with eyes closed, I saw on her bookshelf a little figurine angel. As we were praying, the little figurine became enlarged and spread out her hands to collect the prayers we were praying! I opened my eyes as I saw that the smell was coming from the little figurine angel! That little glass, a transparent little figurine angel was housing a large demon. I rebuked the spirit because I did not want the interference. I said to the Lord, "What is that?" The Lord told me to go to Exodus to the scripture where God told Moses to build the Ark. The Lord said, "When I told Moses to build the Ark of the Covenant and to place the Mercy Seat on top of the Ark and to set the cherubim on either sides of the Mercy Seat, guess what happened? I came and became the life between the cherubim." God set the Mercy Seat on top of the Ark and sat on the Mercy Seat in the Holy of Holies and He became the life between the two cherubim! He said, "Therefore, when you display an image, like a figurine, it might be small like the little figurine angel, but what you're doing is creating something to be occupied by divine life. If you cannot give life to it, *(because when God told Moses to set it up, God became the life between the cherubim)*, the devil will come and visit it."

On another occasion, I went to visit a lady and I spent the night. She had a little figurine angel in her living room. I was sleeping in the living room when in the middle of the night, this little figurine angel became life-sized and began to float between the ceiling and the floor and I looked up and said, "In the Name of the Lord Jesus...!" I rebuked the thing because before I sleep in somebody's house, I always ask, "If I see something do I have permission to rebuke it?" If they say no, I will not sleep there. She had given me permission and I rebuked it. Do you know that at 6 am she woke up and came into the living room, reached out for the little porcelain angel on the bookshelf and took it into her bedroom and went back to sleep. I had seen the thing and rebuked it and she woke up and took it into her bedroom. The Lord said, "You see how my children open themselves up to be afflicted?" People bring things into their homes that have religious sentiments but if you read Deuteronomy Chapter 4, it says you shall not make any image of any likeness of anything, be it in heaven or on earth. The reason God says don't do it is because you're not able to give it life. Graven images speak of creation. When God wanted to make Adam He formed Adam like clay and the next thing God did was breathe into it. That clay became a man; so when you go and cast something in the image of anything and you are not able to give it life as God does, the devil sends the death angel to dwell in that image and he uses that as access to walk about in your home.

Also, there was a lady I used to visit that had a medium size angel with folded wings in her bedroom. If you went into her bedroom, it did not matter how strong you felt before you got in there, you became instantly weak and weary. The spirits of weariness, fatigue and tiredness were in the angel. I told her she needed to get rid of the angel but she said her son gave it to her and I said OK and I left. Some people are very attached to demonic things so until the Lord gives me liberty to speak to a person, I leave people alone with their demons. But, when the Lord gives me permission to speak or do something, that's when I speak or do something because some people are not ready. If you speak out of time or out of season, they will just lash out against you. I've learned from being beat up by Christians with their tongue to keep my mouth shut and let people keep their demons if the Lord has not sent me to speak to them.

***Question #3:*** *What about stuffed animals for children?*

***Mary's Answer:*** **Stuffed animals for children? I don't know. Ask the Lord because if its something you feel is wrong or demonic when you look at it. There are some that you can tell are demonic right away because you can see the spirits looking back at you. Some toys are demonic, not all toys, so you have to play it by ear. For instance, Mickey Mouse can be demonic because it's been idolized. It might look like a little Mickey Mouse but some people have made it into such a big idol in this nation that it can bring evil spirits into your house.**

***Question #4:*** *You mentioned religious figurines like angels. Now what about the cross?*

***Mary's Answer:*** **You know what? I was hoping that no one would ever ask me that question. I used to wear a cross on my neck. One day I went home to Africa because I was seeking deliverance after I came out of the psychiatric hospital. But do you know where the spirit of insomnia that was tormenting me was lugged? It was hiding in that cross on my neck. One day, I remember standing in front of the door in the morning and my mother just lashed out and went after that cross and she yanked it and cast it down and said, "look unto Jesus, don't look to some image." That**

was the end of my wearing a cross. I bought that cross and I went to a Roman Catholic Priest to have it blessed. For those of you that have read my book, _Unveiling the God-Mother,_ when I went for confession after 15 years of absence from the church, I started feeling very religious and the only thing I knew to do was what I did. I went and bought a Rosary and a Cross and took them to the Priest to have them blessed and I wore the Cross on my neck. As far as I was concerned, I had become a Christian again because I was again wearing a Cross and I own a Rosary but I did not know about being born again. I was very grateful to be a Christian again and I wanted to say "thank you" to God so I paid $10 to the Priest and bought a Mass card. I had them say a "thank you Mass" to God on my behalf because that was how I knew to worship and thank God.

I would not wear a cross now. You see, Emperor Constantine of Rome made the wearing of the cross very popular because that was how he became a Christian. He saw a vision or a dream of the cross and so the cross became something he was passionate about and he mandated that when you build the church you set the steeple on top of the house and put a cross on it. In Martin Luther's _Reformation,_ one of the "95 Thesis" that he wrote against was the wearing of the cross. It was the pagans who wore the images of their god's and Christians were beginning to emulate them by wearing the cross. Pagans wore the image

103

of whatever god they worshipped on their neck. Subsequently, when they came into the church Christian's began to wear crosses also. If you wear the cross and you go to sleep at night, you might open yourself up to demonic attack because whatever spirit could not get to you during the day might attach itself to that cross at night and from the cross begin to make contact with your body. You can find yourself always going to the doctor and taking medication because of the Cross that you wear on your neck. Jesus is not the cross and what He died for is not that piece of metal that people wear on their neck. The Cross is an object of reproach and Jesus became the scapegoat that took our reproach and shame upon Himself and died for us on the Cross. It speaks of the crucifixion of the flesh. We are to let "the finished works of Christ" be printed in our hearts and not make an idol out of it.

Wearing the cross came from Christians copying the pagans. The devil knows where he has legal ground but Christian's are very, very passionate about their cross so that is why I was hoping that no one would ask about the cross so I could sail on without ruffling anybody's feathers. It is amazing that today's Christians are back to wearing the cross after Martin Luther wrote against it. They do not truly know the message of the cross; they do not know that the cross speaks of death. Jesus took His cross and died on it, and He said for you to take your cross and die on it

– die to the flesh, die to lust, you die to everything that is not of God. Some people have taken it and made an idol out of it. They have equated being a Christian to wearing a cross, which is idolatry.

*Question #5:* *My question is, going back to the story you talked about the lady that the husband had so many pictures, coming from Africa, we have a lot of cultural things we know as Christians are anti-God, anti-Christ. We know because we know where they come from. Now, being a believer and if one has a spouse that is not a believer and really believes in these things, but the Lord tells us that if he doesn't leave we are to pray for him and emulate Christ so that he can see Christ in us so he can come over. But these things are opening doors to demonic attacks in families. What would you say to someone in that situation because here you're trying to say, "OK, God, I know I don't like this but I am believing your Word, I'm standing on your Word and I'm trusting that the best will come out of this."*

*Mary's Answer:* I've been in that situation because when I got born again, it was so funny because when I went home to Nigeria, I had some friends here in the U.S.A. and I wanted to buy souvenirs for them. I gave somebody $300 and asked the person to buy some African things that I could give to my friends when I got back to the States. Guess what they bought me? They bought me all these carvings, engravings, images and "nice" things. At the time, I was not aware of

105

the danger; all my revelation was of the cross and I didn't extend it beyond that. I was so impressed with their purchases that I wondered what they would be able to do with $1000. By the time I came back, I came back with a business. I was going to churches as a newly born again Christian and I was selling African masks and I was making money. The devil just landed the business on my laps and it was bringing me money. Churches were inviting me to come and sell these things. I would go and sell and go to fairs and make money on the weekends. I thought life was very good.

One day while I was doing a fair, it got to a point that some people were asking me for masks that have actually been used in real life sacrifices. I went and made up some cards and I would tell them that this and that item had been used for such and such sacrifice. It was not true but it brought in more money. The more I wrote about some really horrible sacrifice an item had been used for, the more expensive the item was. So I made money selling these things.

One day, while I was telling a guy about a chair, it was a particular chair – the kind that had a queen sitting on it – I was actually selling it for $5,000. I was trying to sell it to the museum. I had it on display with my showcase pieces and when the guy left the Lord said, "You're my daughter aren't you?" I said, "Yes". Then He said, "How do you think it makes me feel when you're describing to these people some horrible and demonic sacrifices in your effort to sell your carvings?" For the first time, my eyes opened to what I was doing and one day I had a dream. I had fallen into this "never, never land" of masks: some of them were so horrible and vicious that they would jump out from the woods in their attempt to frighten me. In that dream I was returning from wherever I had fallen into and as I was coming the whole road was paved with all kinds of devilish masks. Finally, I looked back and I saw that I was out of the place where they were and into a clean area.

But unfortunately, I had already spoken to my brother about opening a store in Atlanta to sell these horrible things. I had to give up the business and I said to my brother, "You need to leave this business alone!" He did not have the revelation that I had so he refused and he ordered a container load of more masks and other items. I had to live in the same apartment with him and all the items when they came. Before I went to sleep at night, I would bind the spirits in the items. I used to quarantine the spirits in their little corner and forbid them from coming near me at night. I had to be very creative and I would say to the spirits whatever space you have been given is where I want you to operate and you cannot leave there and go find me because the cross is between us.

A person has the right over his or her house so what I do is, when I come to a person's house and I see they have set up an idol in their house, I immediately put the Cross between the idol and myself. I would tell it, "As long as you stay where they keep you and you don't find me or try to make contact with me, I will not cast you out." You can actually put the Cross between you and the forces of darkness until the person is ready to get rid of his or her graven images. When I was praying and fasting for the Lord to deliver my brother from the masks business, He said to me, "By the way, who introduced him to this business?" Since then, I never spoke to him about the business. The Lord also told me that I am not responsible for other people's actions.

Therefore, when you discern a spirit in an item in a person's home, you speak to the spirit saying, "I don't know what covenant has been made with you but I don't partake of it." You can quarantine a spirit to whatever environment your husband has given it to stay. You can exercise authority over the rest of the house. Speak to the spirit as God spoke to the proud waves of the sea, "So far can you go and no more!"

*__Question #6:__ A lot of people shop at thrift stores and they purchase things and bring them home. I know you can plead the Blood of Jesus Christ over those things, but does that last for ever or do you have to constantly everyday keep pleading the Blood* *of Jesus Christ over things you have brought from thrift stores into your house or do you just get rid of them?*

**Mary's Answer:** If you're like me, when I pick up something I can discern the spiritual condition of the previous owner. There was something I purchased from the thrift store and whoever owned it before had cancer. You have to know your legal ground. If you know your legal ground, you can take authority accordingly because you always go back to the covenant made with the item. So whatever you buy from the thrift store, as long as that item itself is not demonic, when you bring it home, you might want to confess: "When I bought this item, I made no covenant with the previous owners. I don't receive any covenant that they made with it before I bought it. Their covenant over this item ended when they gave it away or sold to the store. Therefore, when I picked it up and paid for it, I paid for a clean item." From that time on, you have jurisdiction over that item. You have to terminate whatever jurisdiction or authority the previous owners had over that item before you drive away any spirit that is not of God in the item. But, if you bought something demonic, just get rid of it. We don't bind the devils in demonic items we just get rid of the items.

**Question #7:** *What about pictures?*

**Mary's Answer:** Pictures? You mean people's

pictures or demonic pictures? I recently received a magazine from a popular minister that outlines her work in Asia. She had taken a picture with a little girl in Asia. Man, that little girl was so demonized! When I looked at it, I could see the spirit. I can usually discern the spirit on a person even by looking at the person's picture. Also, there are some spirits that actually attach themselves to pictures. Vanity is a good example. Vanity will attach itself to a picture if it was active in a person when the person took the picture. When I look at the picture, I would see the spirit of vanity and it does not matter if the picture was taken 20 years ago.

Once I went to a lady's house and she had told me that when I see anything demonic in her house, I should let her know so that she can get rid of it. The first time I went to her house, I went upstairs to use the bathroom and a spirit tried to slap me at the top of the staircase and I said to the spirit, "In the Name of Jesus, I send you back your wickedness because I do not receive it!" I did not know what it was and I did not see the spirit but no evil spirit has the right to touch me! I said to the lady, there is no object or image on this spot so what is the spirit at the top of your staircase attached to? I asked her to come up to the area and I told her that a spirit tried to slap me and that I slapped it back with the Word of God. I said to her, "You gave it authority in your house so what was here before?" She told me that she had one of those African masks mounted at the top of her staircase for a while until someone told her to get rid of it. I said to her, "Did you tell the spirit that you had given permission to stay through the mask to leave also?" I told her that the spirit was lingering in her house! The mask left but the spirit did not go with it. It stayed behind. I told her to tell the spirit to go with the mask. We prayed and she commanded the spirit to go and she took back every authority she gave the spirit to stay in that place and we went downstairs to pray.

There was a picture of her behind us as we were praying and when I opened my eyes, her picture was rolling its eyes at me. Her picture! I told her about the picture and I asked her about the story behind the picture. I told her the only time I see pictures rolling eyes like that is when I go down the checkout isle in the grocery store because I can see the spirits of vanity and lust in those magazines. While in the grocery store, I would plead the Blood of Jesus and just keep on moving because if I look at them, they sometimes wink at me or roll their eyes at me with an evil smile. Sometimes, they are almost leaping off the cover of the magazines because the spirit was active when the picture was taken. Therefore, I said to her, the only place I see this spirit that is rolling her eyes is in the grocery store at the checkout area. She said, "It's funny you said that because that's my glamour shot!" She said she had tried to model and that was the picture she was sending to the different modeling houses and other places.

111

Not all pictures are demonic and not all art is demonic because it depends on the spirit behind each. This lady is fine in real life but something was wrong with the picture. Until she told me the purpose for which the picture was taken and the circumstances, I did not understand why vanity had attached herself to her picture.

*Question #8:* *You said that the cross is not a good thing. I have a lot of spiritual pictures in my house and one is with a cross above the man, like a cross over him and he's laying over on the Bible. Is that wicked and do I need to get that out of my house?*

*Mary's Answer:* I don't know. You ask the Lord because I once had a picture of Jesus, the smiling Jesus– Jesus in a hilarious state. I loved that picture of the Lord Jesus and I thought it was a very beautiful picture. I said ok, Lord, "Just this one – I really, really like it." I had it on my wall and it was the only picture on my wall. Do you know that every time I went by it, it would wink at me? It was so funny. When I walked into my apartment and as I would turn to go towards the bedroom, it would wink at me because the spirit of idolatry had attached itself to it. I had to get rid of it. So you have to ask the Lord to reveal to you what is demonic and what is not. Know also that not everybody is as sensitive to spirits as I am but I wish that everyone would be as sensitive as me so they would know what to stay away from. I'm very, very sensitive and my radar is highly sensitized to discern both good and bad spirits.

112

There was a time I could not go to the Mall. There was a time I couldn't be among people because I could see all kinds of stuff. I wanted the Lord to build me a house in the woods so that I could stay away from people and evil spirits. I wanted Him to give me the house and a telephone so I could call whomever I wanted to talk to without having to deal with some people and their spirits. But the Lord said He needed me out in the public.

*Question #9:* *What about if you made ceramics? Ceramic cats and you made them yourself. Would that be demonic?*

*Mary's Answer:* Well, I would refer you to Deuteronomy 4:16-18 and let that answer your question because it says don't make it. Don't make any graven image of any likeness of anything in heaven or on earth. So if you're making it, that's a violation of that scripture, right away. But you have to read it for yourself. Go to the Lord — one of the things I like about the Thessalonians Church is that when they heard things, they looked into the scriptures to check out the accuracy of what they heard. If somebody says something to me I would say, "Lord this person said this… What do you say?" Like the other day, it was just so funny because all of a sudden I drew a blank concerning standing in as a point of contact as they prayed for a friend of mine who was sick in the hospital. They asked me to stand in as they prayed, so I did. I agreed in the prayer when they were praying for this person but when I got home and into the presence of the Lord, it occurred to me that I was not "really clear" about the spiritual principle of standing in as a point of contact for someone as others pray for the person. When I am before the Lord and I'm ignorant about something that I had done, the Lord would show me my ignorance immediately. As soon as I opened my mouth to pray and thank the Father for bringing me home safely, I became aware of my ignorance. I asked the Lord what was the whole purpose of standing as a point of contact for someone in prayer as the others pray. He said, "Child it's called standing in the gap." I said, "What does that mean?" He said, "Remember when the congregation was about to be destroyed and Moses told Aaron to go stand between the Congregation and God so that God would not destroy the congregation? He said, "That is the precedence for what you did." I said, "OK". God wants you to have wisdom and have knowledge in whatever you're doing. He hates ignorance. Therefore, when you hear something, take it to Him and let Him work it in your life so that you can get a revelation because if you do things just because you heard this and that, you're going to be very unstable. You have to be grounded in what you're doing and only the Word of God can help you do this. For instance in reference to this ceramic cat that you made, you have the scripture in Deuteronomy Chapter 4 and you can also ask the Lord. If you're like me, He will let you see what that ceramic cat does in

114

the spirit and then you will have to make up your mind whether or not you want it in your house.

Let the Word of God be your guide because the Holy Ghost leads us, we don't lead ourselves. Don't feel condemned because the Lord will give you more understanding. You do need to let what you have heard bring conviction into your heart but if you feel condemnation after hearing this, we're going to pray that you receive discernment and we're going to ask the Lord to open your eyes so that you can see what your ceramic cats do when you go to sleep. So either they're going to have to leave your house or you're going to leave.

# Chapter 4
# Can a Christian Have a Demon?

When the Lord gave me the teaching in this Chapter, I was so happy. Remember in the beginning I mentioned some of the questions people ask. They are question such as: Are evil spirits and unclean spirits the same as demons? Are evil spirits and demons fallen angels? Are sicknesses and diseases the works of evil spirits, etc.? Also, people tend to frequently ask, "Can a Christian Have a Demon?" This is also one of the areas that the devil has been really able to afflict a lot of Christians because of ignorance and false doctrines. I felt impressed upon by the Lord to make sure that I answer this particular question thoroughly so that when someone asks you the same question, you would be able to give the person the Word of the Lord on the matter. I am basically going to tell you what the Lord taught me regarding this subject.

I love what the late Derek Prince, a great teacher of the Word of God said during one of his teachings on deliverance. They asked him if a Christian can have a demon and he replied: "A Christian can have whatever a Christian wants to have," and it is also my opinion that a Christian can have whatever a Christian allows into his or her life. But I have to address the people who believe that Christians cannot have demons or that evil spirits cannot possess Christians. The reason they say this is because they know that the Holy Ghost took up residence in our spirit when we got born again so to them it is

117

absurd for somebody to say that a Christian can have a demon. Some people really take offense if you say that they have a demon and they are Christians. But when you call for deliverance prayer, they are on the prayer line. The reason for their reaction is lack of understanding of what really went on when they got born again and how their being born again plays out in terms of demonic activity. After reading this Chapter, you should be able to educate those who believe contrary to what is said in this Chapter.

When you got born again, the Holy Spirit came into you; He came into your spirit. Your spirit was renewed you became a new creation in your spirit. But, the Bible says that you should renew your mind. You are to let your mind be transformed by the Word of God because if you do not, your old ways and old habits become doorways or gateways for demonic activities in your life. The devil really comes to you first in your mind. The devil is a trafficker; he will come and sell you an idea and he knows who buys ideas from him. If the devil says to you through thoughts, "Oh, you're depressed" and you say, "Get out. I have the joy of the Lord," he would go to someone else. If he says to the next person, "You're depressed" and the person begin to cry and say, "Oh, I'm depressed," that person becomes the devil's customer. The devil does not know everything; he knows who buys ideas from him and who doesn't. Know that the devil's wicked devices are not aimed at your spirit. He knows that he cannot have your spirit. He is no fool. He knows that your spirit is born again

118

but his wickedness is targeting your mind and your body. He wants to blow your mind and destroy your body. Listen to what he told God in <u>Job 2:4-5</u>:

*So Satan answered the Lord and said, <u>"Skin for Skin! Yea, all that a man has he will give for his life.</u> But put forth thine hand now, and <u>touch his bone and his flesh</u>, and he will curse You to Your face!"*

So you see that the devil's wicked devices are against your flesh and your bones! He believes that when he attacks your bone and your flesh long enough, he can produce his desired effect, which is for you to judge God, blame God and then walk away from God's protection and become an open target; and he (the devil) can then lead you straight into perdition or destruction. He is no fool. He is not aiming for your spirit; he's aiming for your mind and your body. Therefore, those who believe that Christians cannot have evil spirits believe this because they only see one aspect of who we are as new creation in Christ. We are a tri-parted being: we have a spirit, a soul and a body. Actually, we are a spirit beings having a soul and living in a body. Your spirit is fine but it is in your soul and your body that you have your work cut out because God did the work concerning the preservation of your spirit. The devil cannot kill it so he aims for your mind and body. It is your responsibility to protect your mind and body. Those who cannot discern the devil's evil tactic of attacking your mind and body can be deceived into believing that a Christian cannot have a demon.

One thing the devil knows is that a dead Christian is an ineffective Christian. If he can attack your mind and your body and get you out of this earth-realm through physical death, he has nothing to worry about concerning you. As far as he is concerned, you and your spirit can go and be with God but you will not be here on earth to contend with him. Last year when I was coming back from Africa and as soon as I got on the plane on the flight back to the US, the devil said to me through thoughts, "You belong to God, what does it matter whether you live or die?" As soon as I heard that, I knew he was up to no good and I said, "But it is expedient for me to stay right here, right now and not to die!" As I said that, the lady who was to sit in front of me sat down. Immediately the Lord said to me concerning the spirit in the lady, "Rebuke that spirit!" When the flight took off, the spirit in the lady tried to lull me to sleep and it spoke and said, "If you go to be with Jesus, you have nothing to loose..." And it began to try to sell me the thrill of a plane crashing like when you're in a roller coaster. It tried to make me think on how thrilling it would be! Can you imagine that – how thrilling it would be for everything to just be tumbling to destruction! And I said, "Satan, in the Name of the Lord Jesus, you desire the disaster so let it be your portion; I don't buy it!" Our plane just went belly-up; the glove compartment flew open and people were screaming. Never die in a plane crash because it is a horrible thing; you have nowhere to run to and nothing to hold on to. You cannot grab hold of anything; everything is moving and people were screaming. I said, "Father in Jesus Name, I just thank you that I am going to make it to my destination."

In 1997 the Lord showed me how I would exit this world at the appointed time and it was not in a plane crash so I knew that it was not my time to go yet. When the plane came back up, I saw the spirits that tried to cause the plane crash; one was in the lady that sat in front of my seat and the other was in a guy at the back of the plane. I commanded the fire of the Holy Ghost on them to destroy the evil spirits in them because they tried to take out the children of God that were on the plane. I judged the evil spirits by the Word of God.

The devil always aims at your body and your mind so never let anybody tell you otherwise because he is not aiming for your spirit. If you do not believe me that a Christian can have a demon, why are Christians dying prematurely of cancer. Why are they dying of high blood pressure, diabetes, Alzheimer's and why are Christians committing suicide? These spirits are able to attach themselves to your mind and your body if you let them. God gave you the responsibility to protect your mind and your body. I will explain this later. We must be willing to identify the spirits behind the sicknesses and diseases that people wrestle with today in order to do what the Lord commanded us to do, which is to cast them out. Never let anyone tell you that a Christian cannot have a devil because the devils that are coming are coming to attack your flesh and your body. They are not coming for your spirit.

Another thing  I wanted to let you know is that you should never under estimate the devices of the devil. Remember what he said to the Lord in Matthew 4:5-6 when he took the Lord to the pinnacle of the temple.  He said:

*If you are the Son of God, cast yourself down (he wants the Lord to injure himself). For it is written: 'He shall give His angels charge over you.' And 'In their hands they shall bear you up, Lest you dash your foot against a stone.'*

You see, the devil knows scriptures and he read in Exodus that a bone of Jesus' body (the Lamb) shall not be broken so he figured, since no one can break His bones, I can trick Him to break His own bones! This is why he told Jesus, 'Cast yourself down!' He knows that it would be presumptuous on Jesus' part to tempt God the Father by willfully casting Himself down.  If Jesus had obeyed him, He would have broken His own bones and the devil could then say to God the Father, "You said His bones could not be broken but look at Him, He broke His own bones!" The devil's devices have not changed.  He was after the Lord's body and he is after yours. He was after the Lord's mind and he is after yours. Therefore, we have to do what the Lord did—tell him, "It is written…!"

Evil spirits actually help Christians propagate

the false belief that they cannot inhabit a Christian. Scripture tells us, in <u>Ephesians 6:11-18</u> to:

*[11]Put on the whole armor of God that ye may be able to stand against the wiles of the devil. [12] For we wrestle not against flesh and blood, but against principalities, against powers, against the rulers of the darkness of this world, against spiritual wickedness in high places.[13]Therefore, take unto you the whole armor of God that ye may be able to withstand in the evil day and having done all to stand. [14]Stand therefore having your loins girt about with truth, having the breastplate of righteousness, [15]and your feet shod with the preparation of the gospel of peace: [16]And above all, taking the shield of faith, wherewith you shall be able to quench all the fiery darts of the wicked. [17]And take the helmet of salvation, and the sword of the Spirit, which is the word of God; [18]Praying always with all prayer and supplication in the Spirit, being watchful to this end with all perseverance and supplication for all the saints...*

I tell you that the fiery darts are the devil's evil spirits. He sends them out to go afflict the mind and body of anyone who happens to be unprotected. Therefore, I say to you that the extent, to which you put on this whole armor of God as we are directed, is really the extent to which you are protected from satanic attack or demonic invasion or possession. When the devil shoots fiery darts, anybody that has been an archer or has taken archery in school knows that you shoot the darts into something and when it goes, it goes into the target and it leaves a mark. That is why the scripture says that you should put on the whole armor of God. What does it mean to put on the whole armor of God? It means that you must first be born again, renew your mind with God's Word and live by the Word of God because if you are not in Christ, you have no protection. Also, if you do not live by the Word of God, you have no protection.

I asked the Lord why I got afflicted and wound up in a psychiatric hospital and He gave me a vision. Incidentally, the devil is very, very small. He is very small but people magnify him and make him bigger in their mind. He appears to you the way you make him out to be. In this vision, the devil was on the street and the street was deserted. Who else was on the street dilly dallying around? It was Mary and I was ignorant about the devil. He had an old weapon in his hand. He has a mental damage that is beyond description. He is very one-way minded. He does not look back and he has this thing like a shot-gun that has been cut off and he shoots it on either sides of the street indiscriminately. It was as though everybody had taken cover and the houses were all white but I was the only one on the street. He at looked me as if to say, "how dare you be on the same street with me!" He looked at me in order to take a good aim and I was playing on the street because that was what I did in Africa when I was little. If you sent me on an errand and if it was a thirty-minute errand, I made two hours out of it. I went playing and I would kick whatever I could find on the street

124

and dance around and talk to people. They usually sent me to go buy soda for somebody visiting and of course, nobody wanted to touch the soda by the time I came back with it because it was usually too hot! I was doing the same thing in this dream or night vision and before I realized it, there was this entity in front of me that had a little shotgun and was taking a good aim at me. Right before he pulled the trigger, a bride appeared from nowhere in a very white and pure wedding gown and she stood over me with her wedding gown spread over me. She so completely covered me that you could not see me under her wedding gown. The devil was very shocked and I was amazed. Then the scene changed and I saw a group of African soldiers: their title was Soldiers of the Lord. The devil does not look back; he has a one-way mind. These soldiers came from behind him but he could not hear the sound of the wagon coming behind him. I began to look and I saw myself as one of the soldiers in the Lord's army. The wagon pulled up behind him and before he realized what hit him, I jumped out. These soldiers were so efficient that before the wagon came to a stop everybody jumped down. I was the first to reach the devil and I picked him up and I threw him up and raised my leg and cracked him into two pieces and I stepped on his gun. We jumped back into the wagon and drove off.

Afterwards, the Lord began to teach me that the "devil's fiery darts are shot at those who are not protected." When I got born again, people tried to tell me to join a church. I told them, "That is too limiting." Therefore, I went to any church I saw. I was a member of no church. I did not believe in commitment, I believed I should be a free Christian going wherever I wanted. That was also what I was doing in the spirit realm because I was not planted anywhere. Unfortunately when I got afflicted and I was in a mental hospital, none of the pastors of the churches I was visiting came to see me because they said I was not a member of their church. At the time, I was so limited in my knowledge of the scriptures that I asked myself, "Who was the bride with the beautiful white gown that came and spread her white gown over me?" She was so beautiful and bold as she stood over me and the devil left because he was afraid of her.

I shared that vision in order to let you know that it is your responsibility to make sure that the blood of Jesus covers you. He is our whole armor; you have to be in Christ. This is why the scriptures say that: "Ye are dead so your life is hid in Christ with God." You are hid in Christ inside of God. Beyond that, you have to put on the helmet of salvation and renew your mind because the Word of God is what renews your mind. That is your helmet. You have to put on the breastplate of righteousness: everything you do should be done in righteousness. You cannot go about defrauding people, lying, cheating and say that the devil has no hold on you. He will beat you black and blue when he comes into your home. You can go to church and dance on Sunday and go home and suffer loss because he can come in and dwell in your or your home. Have your loins girded about with truth and have your feet shod with the preparation of the gospel of peace. You have to purpose to live at peace with everybody. It is our responsibility to be clothed in this "spiritual dress code" that we have been given because to the extent that you do this is the extent to which the devil cannot have a hold on you. You can be like Jesus when He said, "The prince of this world cometh and he has no place in me" because I am fully clothed! I try to do everything in righteousness by making sure that the Word of God is what I live by. When I miss the mark, I repent but it is my duty to do everything according to the Word of God.

If you study the book of Job, you would note that when satan first came after Job, he looked around in Job's life and saw that there was a hedge around Job and that Job was prosperous. He was vexed but there was nothing he could do. If you do not believe this, look at what he said to God: "Have you not built a hedge around about him? You have prospered him and increased him." Which means the devil once went to Job and he could not do anything to Job. Sometimes I see the devil and I'm like this huge fruitful tree that has so much fruits on it that its branches are almost touching the ground. You can grab whatever fruit you want to eat because they are all ripe. The only entity that I saw who could not get near the tree was the devil. He goes around it but is unable to get to it because it seems as though there is a magnetic field around the tree that repels him away

127

from the tree. I would see him go around and around the tree. Usually, before he comes to the tree, I would hear God the Father say, "Have you considered my servant…?" And I will go, "Oh God, why can't you just leave well enough alone?" I would then say to God the Father, "Is the devil coming?" And He would say, "Oh yes, he's coming and he better not find anything in you." Within two or three days, the devil comes. I would look as he goes around the tree. It might take him almost a week to circle the tree. He would look and look and at last, I would see him put both his hands on his head and begins to cry as he is going away. The other day I woke up to a vision of the devil crying; both his hands were on his head and I told somebody guess what? I'm about to do something really good for God because the devil is crying today! Why? Because we are supposed to make the devil cry and we are to be properly clothed with the whole armor of God so when we go out to do things for God and destroy the works of the devil, we do not become casualties.

Once I asked the Lord, "Why are we not doing the mighty works that you said we are going to do because you said the mighty works you did shall we do also and even greater works. How come we are not doing them?" He said, "Because I'm merciful." I said, "What do you mean?" He said, "My children have so many doors open in their lives for the devil to come and go. If I let them do all the destruction they want to do to the devil and he comes into their house once, he'll take them out." So out of

God's mercy, He makes sure you do not get in over your head because the doors in your life are unprotected but once you allow God to protect you and make sure there are no holes in your armor, then God will unleash you against the devil so you can be a thorn on the devil's side. God told me, "The devil is going to be sorry for the day he tried to come against you." It is my job to make sure that I am properly clothed. It is our job to not live in ignorance and to really take seriously the command that we have been given—put on the whole armor of God and have our whole mind renewed! Again, I say that we are to be transformed by the Word of God as we look into it and as we actually live by it. You can go to church and sing and dance about how much you love Jesus but that is not how Jesus measures how much you love Him. That you go to church, sing, dance and do things for God are not His way of measuring your love for Him. **According to the Lord Jesus, "This is he that loves me; he that obeys my word."** The extent to which you obey the Word of God is the extent to which you love God, no more, no less.

There was a time I watching a man bringing a present to offer before the Lord and of course everybody was awed by what he was doing. He had come to make a public presentation of the harvest from his garden to the Lord. The Lord said, "This is a man who would not obey me, just like Cain—quick to bring the fruit that he planted. But when I tell him to do something, he will not do it but he is coming to make a public show of the love

129

he has for God." And God looks at such things from heaven and says, "Away with this." It is our job to put on the whole armor of God. Take your responsibility serious and keep the fiery darts away from your mind and your body.

Another thing is that a Christian can choose whom to obey. You become a servant of whom you choose to obey. Although you are a Christian, you can choose to obey God or do your own thing, which is really obeying the devil. **Romans 6:16** tells us this:

> **Know ye not, that to whom ye yield your-self servants to obey, his servants ye are to whom you obey. Whether of sin unto death or of obedience unto righteousness.**

He was talking through Paul to the Christians in Rome; they were not unbelievers, they were Christians. You can choose whether you are going to be a servant of righteousness or a servant of the devil even though you are born again. If you do not believe me take a look at what you see in the church today— Christians living like devils, sometimes.

A good illustration of the point I am trying to make here is Adam. When God created Adam, he made him Lord of the whole earth but Adam chose of his own free will to obey the devil and the Bible say that he became a servant of the devil and his generations after him. He is the one that brought us into bondage to the devil by one act of sin—choosing to obey what the devil said rather than what God said. Whom you choose to obey is whom you become the servant of. If iniquity is reigning in your life, you're the devil's servant because sooner or later he's going to get you into sin. But if it is righteousness, Jesus is Lord.

Note this also in **Galatians 4:1**:

**Now I say, That the heir, as long he is a child, differeth nothing from a servant though he be lord of all:**

We are supposed to grow in our knowledge of God as we study His Word. We are to know what God has given us in Christ Jesus. Ignorance is no excuse because the devil can afflict the mind and body of any Christian who lives in ignorance of the Word of God and any Christian who remains a babe. The Bible says that those who remain babes are "unskilled in the Word of righteousness." In other words, they don't know the Word of God and how to use it. People who remain at this level are the ones who believe that you cannot have a devil because they don't know the word of righteousness.

One of the reasons the devil tries to put you out of the earth-realm or attack your mind and body is because he does not want you to be able to bind and cast him out. He does not want you on earth to contend with him, period! A dead Christian is an ineffective Christian to him. He knows he cannot kill your spirit but he can get you out of the earth-realm so you do not spoil his game plan. Once the Lord said to me,

"What do people do when they lose their wallets? Do they not search frantically until they find it?" I said, "Yes." He said the devil is the same way. When a person is born again, he considers it a loss of his own personal property and so just like a lost wallet, he frantically seeks ways to get that soul back. The first thing the devil does is to entice you with your former lusts; the things that you used to lust after will be the very first weapon he uses against you. This is why some people would come to your church, sing, dance and get born again but when you see them two weeks later, they are back to their old ways and you wonder what happened. It is because the devil found them quickly.

If the devil is not able to get that person back, then he tries to hinder the person's walk with the Lord or he tries to distract the person. If he fails at distracting the person in their new Christian walk, he tries to get the person into what we call "religious activities that have no spiritual power." You go to those places where you meet on Sunday, have lunch after service and play bingo and then do it again the following week. Such Christians are no threat to the devil whatsoever and he is happy and they are happy; everybody is happy. Have you ever seen those churches that build their churches and their cemeteries side by side? What a morbid confession. They feast together in the church and every Sunday each persons sees where he or she is going to end up. God forbid! You want to go out there and shake the world for God and not just go from the pew to the cemetery next door. The devil gives inspiration to some Christians in a bad way. When he fails to get you into religious activities with no power, he knows that you are going to become a serious threat to him so his next step is to infiltrate your mind and your body. Now he wants to put you out of commission on earth so you cannot grow up to be a threat to him.

When I look at some people, I could see the Lord in them or the demon in them. Sometimes I can see in a vision that the Lord is bored in a person. He is sitting underneath a tree in the person waiting and this is usually an indication that the person is not giving the Lord anything to work with on his or her behalf. He waits for a lot of people to speak His Word or obey Him so that He can arise on their behalf. One day, I saw the Lord sitting under a tree in me. He had told me to do something that did not make any sense to me and I said, "Lord, how can I do that." So I walked away. Six months later, I saw the Lord underneath a tree in me, just bored. And I said, "Lord, what are you doing?" He said, "Waiting for whenever you choose to obey what I told you to do." I got on the plane and went and obeyed the Lord quickly. It cost me about $600 in airfare that I could have saved if I had just obeyed the Lord when He first spoke to me.

It is our job to choose whom to yield our will to. Choose to always serve the Lord, to know the Word of the Lord and not remain a babe because ignorance is what the devil looks for in order to prosper in a soul. If he looks into you and sees that there is no Word of God in you, then you are no threat to him. The Word of God is what builds faith in us. The children of Israel saw the miracles of God; they watched God thunder from heaven and divide the red sea but they had no faith. Faith is born by hearing the Word of God. It is the Word of God that keeps you when the devil rises up against you. Someone called me the other day and said so and so fell into sin in their Christian walk. I said, yes, because the person did not have the Word in them.

If all you do is sing and dance and you do not spend time to know "what thus saith the Lord," you can fall into sin because when the devil tells you something, what rises up in you by the Holy Ghost is the Word of God in you. If you do not have anything (the Word of God) to give Jesus to work with on your behalf as the scriptures say, "When the enemy comes in like a flood, the Spirit of the Lord will lift a standard against him," He will not be able to fight on your behalf. The Word of God in you is the standard that the Holy Spirit lifts up in you against the devil. Without the Word of God in you, it is only a question of time before common sense and rationale take over your thinking process and the next thing you know, you give into temptation because the devil can wear you out. Purpose in your mind to be mature Christians that live by the Word of the Lord and if someone asks you, "Can a Christian Have a demon?" You should say to the person, a Christian can have whatever a Christian wants to have because our spirits are renewed but we are supposed to renew minds and we

134

are supposed to put on the whole armor of God in order to keep the fairy darts away.

There is one scripture that I did not understand before the Lord gave me this teaching about Christians and evil spirits. It is one of the parables about a man that came to the wedding banquet and did not have on the right jacket and he was cast into outer darkness. It always bothered me because I could not understand why they would cast him out for not wearing the proper jacket. After this teaching, I saw that the man never bothered to find out what the mantle was; in other words, he never got saved. He hung around as a Christian outwardly but he never looked into the Word of the Lord to live by it; he had nothing of the Lord on. When the Lord looked at him, he cast him out because he did not belong to the Lord. When the devil sees that you have on the whole armor of God, he knows. He can take a look at two Christians and see that one has on the whole armor and the other does not—an open target that he can go after. Purpose in your mind to believe that a Christians can have whatever a Christians wants to have.

The following is an example of how the devil can hold Christians bound with ignorance and unbelief. Sometime ago, we visited a deliverance ministry and John went with us. John has spinal bifida so the prophet who was ministering prayed for John and rebuked the spirit of spinal bifida from him. When we came back, John's friend called and said, "Do you know that John was offended?" I said, "For what?"

He said, "Because that minister from Africa dared to rebuke a devil from him. John said that he is born again and spirit filled so how dare the African prophet to think that he (John) has a demon!" I said, "Just do me a favor and ask him if he thinks that it is the will of God for him to be walking around all crooked up? Ask him if he thinks that his condition brings God glory?" It is amazing what kind of doctrines people believe. Wrong doctrines people open for the devil to attack. The devil is very happy when people hold onto their wrong doctrines because he cannot be challenged out of the people's lives because the people will not allow it. They will not allow anybody to deal with the spirits that are afflicting them because their ignorance and false doctrines are holding the demons in place in their lives.

I said all that to tell you that a Christian really can have whatever a Christian wants to have. Any questions?

## Questions and Answers

***Question #1:*** *I have a question about when you come in contact with people that want to quote scriptures to you all the time but in your heart you know they're not serving God the way they should. I also dreamed a bad dream about this person. So, I've been praying and asking God to show me if He's sending that person in my life for me to help or do I need to rebuke this person?*

*Mary's Answer:* To be honest with you, my thing is, is it a judgment in your heart against this person or is it a true discernment? I would start with myself. I would ask the Lord to help me understand if I am perceiving this person rightly because there are some people that when you see them initially, you say, "I don't want to have anything to do with this person." I caught myself doing that last night. I was sitting beside this person in the service and he just had a nasty habit. He just kept clearing his throat and I can hear this horrible phlegm. It was really nasty! His habit was just rubbing me the wrong way and before I knew it, I said, "Do you need a Kleenex?" When you are dealing with people, you have to make sure that there is no judgment in your heart against them in order to have an accurate discernment about them. Therefore, ask the Lord to first reveal your heart to you concerning this person.

*Question #2:* *The first one was a Gospel Channel that I used to watch and it will be on all night and I was thinking that I'll get the Word of God into the atmosphere in my house all night. But one night, I fell asleep and as I woke up and the pastor's face was demonized and I closed my eyes and I opened them again and it was still demonized. I didn't understand it but I haven't watched that program since then.*

*Mary's Answer:* So you were watching a program and fell asleep? Was this a vision or an actual looking into the television and seeing a

**demonized pastor?**

**_Student's Reply:_** *It was actually looking into the television.*

**_Mary's Answer Cont'd:_ I've actually looked at somebody and when I looked at the person, I saw a snake that looked as if it was about to pounce. I could see the "serpentine spirit" that has really swallowed up the person to the point that the snake is almost bursting forth through the person. When you look at TV or pictures, you can see the spirit in the people. If you can discern spirits in the physical, you can also discern them even in photographs or on TV. I believe that the Lord showed you that the person was a man of God that needed to be delivered from evil spirits. The devil had a foothold in the person. What I would have done is pray for the person.**

There was a time when I had a vision of a popular minister. It was as though I went to his house to do dishes. I remember stepping into the kitchen and there was no place to step foot on. The kitchen floor was covered with crocodiles, turtles, snakes, worms, etc. Thing were just crawling on the floor but by some miracle, I got to the top of the counter and I stood on the counter in order to help do the dishes. Also, in this vision, I saw this minister carrying a chip on his shoulder walking around feeling as though everything was so good but reptiles were just freely moving around in his home. The next time I saw the person on TV, he actually had something on is shoulder and was walking around just as I saw in the vision and I said, "Oh my God, help!" So there are times when what you saw in a vision and in the physical through even a TV is an actual diagnosis of the person's spiritual condition.

There are some pastors that I meet and I know that they are not saved from the devil's fairy darts and that they need deliverance. Although they are leading a congregation, they need salvation and deliverance because when I look at them, satan looks back at me through them. It is what I would call diagnosis i.e., God opening the person up so you see what is in the person. Although the person is in the ministry, the person is not really for the Lord yet. You should pray rather than run from that channel. I would have found out the name of the pastor so that I could begin to pray salvation and deliverance for him rather than run away. Usually, when you are a beginner in the deliverance ministry, the things you see make you want to run away in fear.

During my very first spiritual encounter, I wanted to run because I was not prepared for what happened. Nobody even told me about spirits manifesting. I went from being a Catholic to being saved and I was doing the "spiritual hobo," i.e., going from church to church without belonging to any. I was moving back to Georgia and I went to tell a lady that I knew about Jesus and salvation. I said to myself that, if the last thing I did for her was lead her to the

Lord, it would be great because she was a nice lady. I was very naïve and I did not even pray before going to see her. As soon as she met me at the door, the Holy Ghost said, "Don't hug her!" (One of things the Lord gave me to help me out in my phase of "zeal without knowledge" is the ability to hear instruction). As a result of the instruction from the Holy Spirit, I held my pocketbook to my chest because that is the one way I can prevent bodily contact with her. I did not hug her and I noticed she was not even attempting to hug me either and it made me feel better. So we walked into the living room and I saw that her arm was black and blue. It was summertime and she had on a sleeveless t-shirt. I said to her, "What happened to you?" She said, "I fell." I said, "You fell from where?" She said from her bed. I thought how strange, and I wondered how someone could fall from a bed and be that black and blue. It did not make any sense to me. I did not waste any time as to why I came to see her so I told her that I came to tell her that Jesus has done so many wonderful things for me and I wanted her to receive the same type of blessings. She kept telling me that she was Catholic. For everything I would say to her, she would say, "I'm Catholic" and she became inflated in size! My first reaction was to head for the door but I made a decision not to fear the spirit. When I did, the Holy Spirit came and stood between the lady and me. He said to me, "Call her by her name." I called her by her name and she deflated! Throughout my conversation with her, whenever she would inflate, I would call her by her name and she would deflate. I was very sad because she would not receive the message of salvation and eventually I had to leave. When I got outside the door I said, "Oh, God I thank you!" I did not know what the spirit was until I came back to Georgia. I had that spiritual encounter but I was still ignorant about the spirit. One day, I was walking towards a lady and she also began to expand and contract just like the lady in New York and I was like, "Oh, no, not again!" This time, I was not afraid as at the first time. The Lord dealt with that fear. As I watched her expand and contract, I wanted to know what the spirit was. The Lord said to me, "watch her." Somebody had brought in a birthday cake to the office and she was going to cut a piece and she was almost dancing! The Lord instructed that what I was looking at was the spirit of gluttony (obesity). When it sits on a person, the person does not feel full after eating a large portion of meal. It makes the person to eat and eat and it expands the person for more and more food. This is why the people who are afflicted by obesity get so big because they cannot feel full. There are times that you have to ask the Holy Ghost to let you know when you are full. When you are battling that spirit, you can eat ten plates of food and you do not feel full because that spirit keeps expanding you for more, and more. If you are going to minister in the United States, know that this is one of the spirits that you initially have to overcome. It has a big-time assignment against a lot of people in this country. Therefore, when I'm ministering deliverance to someone and I see the person begin to expand and contract, I would go, "Obesity, in the Name of the Lord Jesus, loose the person." The Lord will help you to build your own spiritual vocabulary with your spiritual encounters.

*Question #3: This happened recently. I was in the bed and I had fallen asleep. I know I hadn't been in the Word like I should have but two spirits came as I woke up. They were two spirits flying at me and one came at me and was choking me and I started coughing. I didn't know if it was because of someone I had been talking to or trying to help. I don't know if it had been an attack from that or what it could have been. Today, I learned a lot about the images because I have a lot of picture of angels and even in my room I have a big carpet with two baby angels. I didn't know if it was because of that.*

*Mary's Answer:* **I had an encounter with the choking spirit. That is why I know that it is not a good thing for someone to die in his or her sleep. It is most horrible for a person to die in their sleep because when that spirit came against me, it elbowed me from behind and with one scoop tried to twist and snap off my neck. When a person is under the grip of this death spirit, the person's legs go limp while the person is trying to scream because the spirit cuts off the person's air supply so that the person actually suffocates. The first time I had an encounter with that spirit was when I was coming to Georgia. I did not know the call of God upon my life. I was moving to Georgia initially in order to set up my African masks busi-**

ness. I remember that my brother called me and told me that they were on their way to come get me in Albany. They were driving up from Georgia to New York. That evening I went to sleep at 6:00 pm because I had just returned from Africa and therefore was still adjusting to the time change. When I left Africa to return to Albany, New York about four days prior, my spirit latched onto the scripture that says, "He that liveth and believeth on me shall never die," and it wouldn't let it go. I found myself subconsciously saying this scripture until I began to verbalize it. When the spirit of death came flying into the room where I was sleeping at about 6:00 pm, it said, "Oh short lifespan is something to be desired. Who cares whether or not you live your full life." It was just talking as it went for my neck from behind to snap it off. This was one of the days that I knew and I knew that God has given me a fighting spirit. My spirit cried out, "Jesus, Savior, Redeemer, Master!" Do you know what happened? As we go about our daily chores, we do not really comprehend the full extent of the power of the Holy Ghost that is in us. On this day, I knew that I carried the Holy Ghost inside of me. I also did not know the extent of the power that the Lord gave me when He raised me up from the dead. He imparted to me the resurrection fire and heat of the Holy Ghost that raises a frozen cadaver. That heat is over 2000 degrees hot and it is what keeps our bodies warm. Therefore, when the spirit attacked me and I called on the name of the Lord Jesus, He just let the fire loose and I watched the arm of the death spirit that was around my neck shrink from a whole hand to nothing! It became just a little thing that was dangling and it was limp! That spirit lost that arm and I was like, "Oh my God what an awesome power that the Lord Jesus has." When it was leaving, it had no more arm and I said, "That's what you get for trying to mess with me!" That was how I first encountered the death spirit and do you know that when I went to pray for someone last week the death spirit tried to attack me again and guess what I saw? I saw that little stump of an arm and I said, "Oh Lord, thank you!" The devil was no longer effective against me with death because he tried to come again but he had no arm.

Also, once the spirit of stroke came against me. The spirit of stroke is like a bird. It is a dirty red bird. What it does is that it aims for a nerve somewhere on someone's neck and it just pecks it and severs it. A few days or months later, you would hear that the person had a stroke. When it came about two years ago to peck my neck, it was not prepared for the fire of God in me. I was like, "Man, I'm hot in the Spirit!" When that beak tried to peck my neck, the fire of God that is on me burnt away the beak and it had no more beak! I said, "Serves you right! See you guys should obey the scripture that says, 'Touch not my anointed...'" As you overcome evil spirits, you begin to learn natures and habits of evil spirits and how the Lord wants to use you to help people overcome them also. From this experience, I found that lot of people limping or paralyzed on their left side had been attacked by the spirit of stroke. When you see a bird flying against you in the nighttime, rebuke it because witches turn into birds and fly against people at night. This is why sometimes when you go to sleep you feel something pressing you down and you are trying to scream. When this happen, it means that you are dealing with witchcraft spirits; there is an assignment against you and sometimes you can scream and sometime you cannot scream. If you stay in the Word of the Lord enough, your spirit will cry out, "Jesus." If your Word level is low (not spending time in the Word of God), you would not be able to scream or move. Not being able to scream or move when witchcraft spirits are pressing you on your bed tells you that your Word level is low. When that happens, I go into the scriptures and feed on the Word of God because you have to build your spirit man up so that it can be strong and able to cry out to the Lord when there is danger.

***Question #4:*** *I had a dream and actually when I woke up from the dream, I saw the manifestation of a lady in my room. But, in the dream it was the lady and a little boy and they were walking. The lady tried to feed me something and when she gave it to me, it was like I ate it but then I threw it out and it was still whole. Then I took the thing and I put it in a drawer and then the lady and the little boy were coming down the hallway (they never talked out loud) and*

*the little boy went and showed the lady where I put
the thing in the drawer and he pulled the drawer out.
And then, I guess maybe I was just crying out and
my husband was trying to wake me up. When I was
coming out of the dream, I saw the manifestation of
the lady in my room.*

***Mary's Answer:*** You were dealing with witchcraft spirits because witches feed you things in the
dream. That is how they bring sickness against
people. The devil always tries to make you receive
the evil that he wants to bring against you. Therefore, when you find yourself eating things that are
not clean in the dream, know that it's the work of
witchcraft and familiar spirits because the devil
cannot attack you unless you open the door with
your mouth for him. When he comes, he brings a
spirit that looks like you. The spirit will be doing
all these things in the dream as though he or she
is you and the minute you say that what you saw
was you, it becomes you because you received the
package from the familiar spirit. That's how he
uses familiar spirits. That is why when you know
that you are Spirit- filled and doing all the good
things and you have a dream in which you see the
opposite of who you know you are, when you wake
up in the morning, you say, "In the Name of the
Lord Jesus, I thank you Father that was not me.
I do not receive that familiar spirit; I send back
that assignment to where it came from. I thank
you that I'm born again and spirit filled." Confess
righteousness because the devil uses a lot of famil-

146

**iar spirits as baits to make you believe in a familiar spirit that looks like you. As you grow in discernment, when you look at that image that looks like you, believe it or not there will be something that is different between you and that image. There is some aspect in which, if you're born again, the devil cannot counterfeit. There will be a distortion of you somewhere in that whole image if you look at it closely because it is a familiar spirit and not you.**

Prayer to cancel the assignment of the spirit of witchcraft: If you're from Africa, the witchcraft level in Africa is more involved and very, very structured. A person can be a witch and fly from Africa as a bird into your house at night, either to peck you or do something to you and go back because there's no distance in the spirit. That is why in Africa when it sounds as though someone is calling your name and you turn around and you do not see anybody, you reject the call. Do you know what an African does in this case, they would say, "That was not my name that was just called" but in America, the people would go, "Did anybody just call me? I thought I heard someone calling me." The reason the Africans reject the call is because they know that when the spirit of witchcraft is sent to kill you, it first has to call you by name and you must reply before it can kill you. Because the Africans know that, when they hear their names and they do not see the person calling them, they would reject the call because they know the spiritual principle. The devil cannot give

147

you anything unless you first receive it either in a vision or dream or any other way such as false doctrine and wrong teaching. We are going to reject the food but first of all, you are going to declare that that was not you in that dream. You are going to send the whole package back to the devil. The Word of God says that we are created in righteousness unto good works so when you see the devil trying to represent you as being created to the contrary, say, "No, no, and reject the package and send it back to him.

### _Mary Prays for student and says, Repeat after me:_

_"Say, Father God, in the Name of the Lord Jesus, I thank you that I am made in your image, born of Your Holy Spirit and washed with the Blood of Jesus. I thank you Father that what you have not fed me spiritually and physically, even in dreams I have not eaten. I reject all demonic food and the spirits behind them. I send back the assignment to the sender because the Word of God says, 'He that digs a pit shall fall into it.' So I command that spirit and every entity that sent that assignment of evil feeding against me to fall into that destruction. As for me, goodness and mercy shall follow me all the days of my life. I shall live and not die and I shall feed on the Word of God forever. In the Name of Jesus." So be it in Jesus Name._

### _Mary Prays:_

_"Father, we thank you that every assignment of witchcraft against her to feed her evil in her sleep shall not happen, in Jesus' Name. We cancel it in the_

*Name of Jesus and we thank you Lord that she shall feed from your Word, feed from your Spirit in Jesus Name. No demonic food shall be in her dream henceforth forever, in Jesus Name." Amen.*

Never see yourself eating something that is not clean in a dream and not do anything about it because if you do, you are going to get sick in the physical. The devil has to feed it to you, he has to give you something and get you to receive it, be it in a dream or any other way that he can give it to you. He will try but you have to resist him. When you find yourself eating something unclean in a dream, when you wake up, you need to say, "That's not me. God I thank you that I did not eat the unclean thing because that is a familiar spirit try to be me. I put a distance and I put the cross between me and that unclean spirit and I send the familiar spirit back." When you do this, you will not get sick.

__*Question #5*__*: How do you know if a spirit is inside or outside a person and what do you do when a spirit rises up against you from another person?*

__*Mary's Answer*__*:* The anointing to discern spirits is what shows you whether a spirit is inside of a person or outside of a person. I was praying for someone the other day and the person's spirit rose up against me and tried to attack me and I commanded the fire of the Holy Ghost to burn up the spirit that rose up against me. The Word of God says, "Touch not my anointed and do my prophets no harm." So any spirit that comes against me or against any believer or any one of you, violates that scripture. You can punish the spirit. When I commanded the fire of the Holy Ghost to destroy that spirit, do you know what came out of her? The whole Statute of Liberty just walked out and I saw her walking away with her little torch. That was the idolatry spirit in her! I do not how she came in contact with it but that was what it was. I see by the power of the discerning of spirits whether the spirit is in the person or attached to the person. Usually, I go by the scripture, "The eye is the window to the soul." There are some people that when you look at them, it is the devil that looks back at you through them. There are some people that I've known for years and years and I'm yet to see the real person. Even though I meet them just about every time, I am yet to see the real person that they are because when I look at them, I see the evil spirit that is oppressing them. Every time I look at them, I see the demon in them because that is what looks back at me. Because God has not told me to minister deliverance or do anything, I just love them and pray that the Lord would lead them to where they can be delivered. Sometimes He would move upon someone to share his or her plight with me saying, "I'm dealing with this and that." I would then ask the Lord if it is a good time to tell the person what I have been seeing in him or her. The person might say, "You mean for all this time you have known this? How come you never told me?" I would say, "Because I have to wait until the Lord is ready to deal with it." I'm not my own sender; the Lord is my sender so I have to go when I'm sent. You can get beat up by evil spirits when you do not know what you're doing or when you act presumptuously. Usually the eyes will tell you if there is a spirit in there. You can look at the spirit and the spirit that is looking back at you can even flash you. When a spirit flashes me through a person, I have to cut the spirit down with the Word of God. I will quote a scripture against any spirit that flashes me through a person. I do not say to the person, "You need deliverance." You have to be led by the Holy Ghost when it comes to the ministry of deliverance. When you look at a person and you can discern an evil spirit in the person or hear an evil spirit speaking through the person, you can cut the spirit down with the Word of God and shut it up.

To answer another student's question about someone fastening something to you or against you, all you have to do is cancel every assignment that you perceived has been sent against you. For example, someone was supposed to come and take a look at my AP system last Monday. A friend of mine said, "I don't think we should let him look at the system." When I went to lie down, this person had all kinds of stuff attached to him. He had pots, pans, bags, luggage and many other things attached to him and he was on his way to my house. I discerned that it was

151

an assignment against me. The person was on a mission from the devil against me and I said, "Oh no you don't!" I prayed, "Father every covenant of coming to my house that I made with this person, I cancel it right now and I stop him from coming. I take back that invitation that I gave him to come to my house." After I prayed, he never called me and he never showed up to this day. Praise God! Once you take back your legal ground in the spirit, you control what happens in the physical. If I had not known what to do and that person came to my house, when he leaves, all kinds of things will begin to happen in my house. I have enough to contend with in my life. I do not need extra baggage, pots and pans coming from somebody that I do not even know. Neither did I go over to the person and say, "Oh you need deliverance!" I will not do that if the Lord has not instructed me to. Some people might not be ready for what you discern in them. The Lord has to prepare them to receive deliverance. If you met 10 people and you can find three (3) clean people among the 10, you're doing really well. That's how bad it is.

# Chapter 5
# How to Identify Evil Spirits

You may be wondering, "Why do we really want to bother ourselves to learn how to identify or how to expel evil spirits?" Well, we have already laid the foundation that you have to believe that evil spirits exist. We cannot pretend that they do not exist because they are your enemies and they are out to destroy you and if you don't take them seriously they can really do you harm, and we do not want that. If you go after them, you have to go after them according to the Word of the Lord. You do not go after evil spirits in ignorance because if you do, you can cause harm to yourself and harm to others. Incidentally, I want you to look at the following news article that I printed out from the Internet about the Romanian Orthodox Church. The headline reads:

***Romania Stunned by Nun's Death in Exorcism***
A Romanian nun died because the Orthodox Convent in Romania has a priest there that supposedly does exorcism. Him and some other nuns were trying to deliver the nun from an evil spirit but their actions resulted in the death of the nun. The article reads:
Last week, Cornici (the nun) was bound to a cross, gagged with a towel and left in a dark room at the convent for three days without food -- where she died of suffocation and dehydration. The case has stunned this impoverished nation where rural youths, many raised in orphanages like Cornici, have flocked to Orthodox monasteries and convents for spiritual

help or food and shelter. Polls show the Orthodox Church to be the nation's most trusted institution. In April, Cornici was admitted to a psychiatric hospital in the northeast city of Vaslui. "She thought the devil was talking to her and told her that she was a sinful person," said Dr. Gheorghe Silvestrovici, a psychiatrist who treated her. "It's a symptom of schizophrenia, and she was probably having her first episode. "The nun was given medication and released on April 20 to the care of the Holy Trinity convent in the nearby village of Tanacu, an isolated community of about 1,000 people in a hilly area cultivated with vineyards and corn. She was supposed to return in 10 days, but never did...

The article then goes into how the priest decided she was possessed because she said she was hearing the devil and they then tried to perform this exorcism on this poor nun and killed her instead. As you can see, this is one instance of how not knowing what to do when you are dealing with evil sprits could do more harm than good. Therefore, if you are wondering why we are having classes such as this one, this is one of the reasons. If you are going to go after the devil, make sure you are doing it according to the Word of the Lord.
**Hebrews 5:13-14**, says:

> [13] *For every one that useth milk is unskilful in the word of righteousness: for he is a babe.* [14] *But strong meat belongeth to them that are of full age, even those who*

*__by reason of use have their senses exer-
cised to discern both good and evil.__*

The Bible says that milk is for babes, but
strong meat is for those people who are willing to
have their senses exercised. That is why you cannot
be afraid of the devil or let the devil intimidate you
and run you off concerning the ministry of deliverance. This Chapter is how to identify evil spirits. In
order for you to do this, you have to acquire skills
and really let the Holy Ghost raise you up and teach
you what you are supposed to do once you have identified them.

We do not want to remain babes; neither
do we want to be afraid of the devil because Jesus
has already defeated the devil for us. He said to us
repeatedly "fear not." Why? Because He knows the
devil will try to instill fear in you when it comes to
evil spirits. I say to you again that Jesus has defeated
the devil and He has given us authority and He wants
us to exercise that authority over the devil and we are
to reign over the evil spirits. We have the power to
cast them out.

Many people are afraid and a lot of people
also refuse to relate the reoccurring events that
happen in their lives and in the lives of their friends
and relatives to the works of evil spirits. They do
this because they are afraid or ignorant about the
activities of evil spirits. As a result, the activities of
evil spirits in their lives go unchallenged for many

months or years. Some people live all their lives in
defeat because the evil spirits assigned against them
by the devil always manage to hinder the progress in
their lives. Therefore, these people live in poverty,
unemployment, sexual sin, sickness and diseases and
other various types of sorrows. This is the reason
God said in **Hosea 4:6**:

*⁶My people are destroyed for lack of knowledge...*

That nun was destroyed because of lack of knowledge. If that priest had known what he was doing,
she would be alive today. It was not God's will for
her to die the way she did. God does not want us
to live in ignorance. He told us in **John 8:12**:

*¹²Then spake Jesus again unto them,
saying, I am the light of the world: he that
followeth me shall not walk in darkness, but
shall have the light of life.*

God wants you to know what He has for you. He wants
to illuminate you by using the Holy Spirit to teach you
His Word, His ways and to also reveal to you the ways
of the devil so you would not be ignorant.

Now that we have a good knowledge about
some of the activities of evil spirits as we have discussed in Chapters 3 and 4, what we now want to
know is how to identify these activities. To answer
these questions, we have to look into the Bible. We
established in Chapter 1 through Chapter 3 that God

is a good Spirit and that the devil is a bad spirit, and that we need to be able to identify the devil and his demons and to cast them out. We must always remember that in any situation, the Word of the Lord is the only truth in the situation. It is not your feelings, it is not your experience and it is not what someone tells you but "what thus saith the Lord." Anything you see, anything you encounter and even anything that anyone is going to tell you cannot contradict the Word of the Lord. If it contradicts the Word of the Lord, you are to say, "No" to it because the Word of God is the yardstick with which we measure and test every spirit. Remember the scripture says, "Test every spirit"? Our instrument for testing every spirit is the Word of God and nothing else. This is why Jesus said in **John 17:17:**

> *[17]Sanctify them through thy truth: thy word is truth.*

We always have to hold on to this scripture that the Word of God is the truth no matter what. There are several ways you can hear from the Lord. Our discernment can come from getting a Rhema word from God or a revelation as you study the Word of the Lord. God can supernaturally tell you or show you evil spirits that have been assigned against you or He can have somebody come up to you and say, "I was praying and the Lord showed me an assignment that has been sent against you. I want to pray with you to break it off you so that you can walk in freedom."

157

Jesus came that we might have life and life more abundantly.  When you are bound up and you are sick or suffering from diseases, you are not having an abundant life nor are you living for the glory of God. Your life is not testifying at that time that God is good because you are busy fighting off devils that you are supposed to put under your feet.  I say that sometimes God in His desire to have us be able to distinguish the good spirits from the bad spirits will allow you to wrestle with evil spirits so you can learn how to identify their ways.  He does not send the evil spirits against you, but in His wisdom, He allows you to wrestle with them because He wants you to be able to discern that which is of Him from that which is not of Him.  That is why in **Hebrews 5:14** says:

*14But strong meat belongeth to them that are of full age, even those who by reason of use have their senses exercised to discern both good and evil.*

How do you exercise your senses?  The Lord once said to me while I was moaning about a situation that I was going through, "Warriors are made in the battleground and not in the living room."  I realized that He is right. You do not stay in your living room and receive a gold medal that announces that you are suddenly a warrior or that you are a general in the army.  You earn a stripe or a medal for every victory you gain over your enemy.  God is not raising an army of wimps.  He wants to raise up a class of people that are strong warriors and He wants to put a rod in their spine so that He can unleash them against the devil. We are the people that God wants to raise up. He wants the devil to cry whenever we step into a place because we are out to do him harm just like he was out to do us harm. We are to turn the table against him.

We actually wrestle against evil spirits. We do not have to shy away from the topic of evil spirits because whether or not you admit that they are here, they are. God wants our spiritual senses to be exercised. I say to you also that the devil knows which Christians have wrestled with him and have defeated him. This is why **Acts 19:15** tells us about the reaction of the evil spirit to the vagabond sons of Sceva:

*[15]And the evil spirit answered and said, Jesus I know, and Paul I know; but who are ye?*

The evil spirit knew that the sons of Sceva had never been in a wrestling match with him and that they were not of the Lord but they came from nowhere to adjure and to bind him. Then the spirit beat them up and stripped them naked. This is why we need to earn some stripes by being willing to be in the battlefield. We have to be willing to confront the demons that are sent against us in order to cast them out. Sometimes the Lord would show me that I have earned a stripe on my military uniform.

I earned my first stripe when I went to witness to an individual. I did not know that the

159

person only had a few days to live. When I turned the corner to go to the house where he lived, the Lord put a stripe on my Army uniform. I said, 'Oh, thank you Lord" but I did not know that I was going into a battlefield. When I reflected on what happened, I said, 'OK, I think I earned that stripe. Thank you Lord." I later earned a star on my military uniform when I snatched another soul from the jaws of spiritual death in Africa. Again, I did not know that the soul was on the verge of death at the time. When I came back, He gave me a star. I became a one-star general when I got back from the trip to Africa. I say this to encourage you to really do damage to the kingdom of darkness. I told somebody that I woke up twice last month in time to see that the devil had both his hands on his head and was crying. I said, "thank you, Lord!" He has vexed my family and I long enough. It is about time we begin to vex him. This is what God wants— for you to be the one that makes the devil run and that makes him cry.

I am now going to give you some points on ways you can personally identify evil spirits. The following are situations; conditions or activities that we need to analyze in order to see if they are the works of evil spirits.

**1.   Attacks in your thought life:**
a. I said earlier that the devil is not after your spirit but your mind and your body. He knows that he cannot have your spirit. This is why we

160

are told in **I Corinthians 2:16** that we have the mind of Christ:

*<sup>16</sup>For who hath known the mind of the Lord, that he may instruct him? but we have the mind of Christ.*

One day, I was confessing over and over that "I have the mind of Christ" and the Lord knew that I had no idea what it means to have the mind of Christ so He asked me, "What is the mind of Christ?" I suddenly realized that I did not know what it means to have the mind of Christ. I was so shocked to find out that I did not know what it means to have the mind of Christ! When He saw that I could not answer the question, He said to me, "The mind of Christ is the Word of God." As believers, our thoughts are supposed to be dominated by the Word of God. Because they are to be pure and holy but when evil spirits are at work in a person's life, they continually inspire the person to think **ungodly thoughts**. This is why some people are in a battle of constantly binding and rejecting evil thoughts. The devil wants to blow your mind. Therefore, when you have repented of any known sin in your life and in your family and you still cannot get victory over impure thoughts and desires, you are most likely dealing with evil spirits. The devil is trying to build a stronghold in your mind. The devil sends evil spirits to hold men's minds captive. Why? Because **Proverbs 23:7** says:

*<sup>7</sup>For as he thinketh in his heart, so is he*

161

The devil knows that if you think it long enough, it is only a matter of time before you actually do it. This is why he insists on you thinking on things that are not good and things that are not pure. He wants you to make that move or that decision to perform an act of sin because when you perform an act of sin, you get into trouble with God. Also, the devil inspires people to think evil thoughts so that he can continually tell them that they are still the same unclean and unworthy people that they were regardless of their salvation because he wants to beat them down. If he can continually get you to think ugly, then you will look at yourself and think "Oh I wonder if I'm really truly saved? Why can't I think right? Why can't I do this? Why can't I do that right?"

b. Sometimes, I go to places and I walk by someone that carries the spirit of lust, you will be surprised what comes out of them. All kinds of sexual, ugly things. Here you are in the grocery store reading some label on a jar or something and someone is walking by and the spirit in the person is just verbalizing all kind of horrible things. If you do not know your own thoughts and who you are in Christ, you might think that the ugly thoughts are yours. When this happens, I just turn around and rebuke the spirit and tell it, "It is written: The wicked shall be silent in darkness." This scripture that I quote against them is from **I Samuel 2:9**:

*⁹He will keep the feet of his saints, **and the***

*__wicked shall be silent in darkness__; for by strength shall no man prevail.*

c. There are people you pass by even in grocery parking lots and the spirit in them is a sexual, devilish or monitoring spirit. I was getting out of my car in the parking lot of a grocery store the other day when the spirit in a guy who was getting into his car began to speak and it said, "Oh you are a publisher" in a mocking way. The guy did not know me from Adam, but the spirit in him, which is a **monitoring spirit** was speaking to me in a mocking way. I said, "You monitoring spirit, I command you to be silent in darkness." I also commanded the fire of the Holy Ghost to deal with the spirit because it had no business monitoring and ease dropping on my conversations. I had just finished a conversation about my publishing company with someone on another side of town before going to this grocery store. I then realized that the person that I had the conversation with carried a monitoring spirit. Her spirit immediately reported our conversation to the evil spirits. Sometimes you wonder why when you plan to do something and you speak about it to someone, the thing gets attacked. You just wonder how it happened. For instance, if you have a job interview and you are so sure that you are going to get the job and you speak it to somebody who carries a monitoring spirit, you have just made a spiritual broadcast of your impending blessing. This is how the devil finds out about your plans and how he knows where to attack you. If you have people who are walking in jealousy towards you, the monitoring spirits informs the spirit of jealousy in them: "Guess who is about to prosper?" They then team up to try to sabotage the prosperity. So, if you have been wondering why your plans seem to be attacked and spoiled by the enemy before they materialize, examine your life to see whom you have been speaking your plans to. You may have been speaking to people that carry ease dropping spirits.

**2. Doctrine of Devils:** The Word of God tells us in **I Thessalonians 5:24**:

*[24] Faithful is he that calleth you, who also will do it.*

Evil spirits preach false doctrines and they inspire unbelief about the faithfulness of God. They will remind you of the things that you have been asking God to do for you that have not yet come to pass. They will then inspire you to believe that God has let you down. They want you convinced that God answers the prayers of every body else but He ignores yours. Evil spirits like to plant evil in your head about God. This is why Paul said in **2 Corinthians 19:5**:

> *"Casting down imaginations, and every high thing that exalteth itself against the knowledge of God, and bringing into captivity every thought to the obedience of Christ."*

You have to bring every thought into captivity to

the Word of God. It is not every thought that flies into your mind that you should receive and it is not every thought you think is born of your spirit. You have to know your thoughts from those that are not yours. An evil spirit can wake you up or alert you during the day and remind you of how you never succeed in the things that you try to do or how nothing good seems to be coming your way lately. It will tell you how everybody else is prospering but you seem to have been left out. Why? Because it is trying to get you beaten down so that the other network of evil spirits can come in for a kill. When you discover an ungodly thought pattern coming your way, immediately recognize it as strange and cast it down. I can close my eyes and if someone that carries a contrary spirit is passing by, I can usually tell. It is amazing how the demons like to send evil thoughts to people and how they do not shut up. There was a time that I was in a clothing store and a spirit was quoting Islamic verses and other evil thoughts directly behind my neck and I turned around and there was a woman covered up from head to toe standing directly behind me and with her head tilted towards me! I commanded the fire of the Holy Ghost upon the spirit in her and I said, "I command the judgment of God upon you for sending evil thoughts against me." I commanded the fire of God upon the woman to kill the evil spirit because the wicked spirit should be silent when I come into a place. The Word of God also says in **Proverbs 14:19** that:

165

*The evil bow before the good; and the wicked at the gates of the righteous.*

Any evil spirit that speaks when you are around, you have the right to pronounce judgment upon. We are the ones reigning in the Name of Jesus and they are to be silent. Watch out for strange thought patterns in your life and even in people that you have conversations with and you will be surprised at how some of them seem to have a negative or evil pattern. When you say something to people with negative thought patterns, the first thing that comes out of their mouth would make you ask, "Where did that come from?" It is a demon that inspires them to see the negative in everything. They cannot see the positive in anything.

**3. Insomnia:** Another way that evil spirits will afflict a person (this they do a lot) is through insomnia, unrest and anxiety. The Word of God tells us in **Psalm 127:2** that God gives His beloved sleep.

> *²It is vain for you to rise up early, to sit up late, to eat the bread of sorrows: for so he giveth his beloved sleep.*

The devil sends his evil spirits as fiery darts to harass, vex, torment and disturb people in the night time in order to make them weary and unable to focus their attention on anything significant during the day. He uses this against people who pray a lot because he knows that if you do not sleep well at night, you cannot focus during the day. When your rest is disturbed, nothing else works right so you cannot be an effective tool against him. If you get an attack at night after you have prayed during the day, then learn how you can commit your spirit, soul and body into the hands of God the Father before you fall asleep so that your sleep can be sweet. Also, ask the Lord to destroy any spirit that will seek to harass you or vex you while you sleep. Pray against witchcraft spirits— they come early in the morning from 3-4 o'clock until 6 o'clock in the morning to try to do evil against people. When you know that you are tired and you had worked hard during the day and you cannot get a decent sleep at night, chances are you are dealing with evil spirits that have been assigned against you. Usually when I pray **Psalm 91** and I repent of anything that I know I have done and I still cannot go to sleep, I would ask the Lord to let me know the covenant that I had made that is allowing the attack.

One time I asked the Lord to show me the covenant a spirit was using to keep me from being able to sleep and it turned out to be a business card that someone gave me. As soon as I asked the Lord to show me the legal ground, He gave me a vision of the business card on my pillow! I thought it was just a business card but the Lord said, "Yes, but he gave you what he had. He had insomnia, that's what he imparted onto the card." I got rid of it. About three months ago, I heard that the guy died and he was only in his late 40's or early 50s. I was not surprised

167

because I knew he was not sleeping at night.

Also, another incident, this happened when Bishop T. D. Jakes was here in Atlanta and I went with a friend. Sometimes it does not pay to be cheap. I did not want to pay for parking and we went to the Doraville Train Station because of free parking. We found free parking and as we were leaving the parking lot, a lady wound down the window of her SUV and handed me a MARTA ticket and she said, "Are you going to Bishop T. D. Jakes' meeting?" I said, "Yes." She said, 'Here, I'll give you this free MARTA card so you don't have to pay for MARTA going and coming. I said, "Praise you, Jesus!" I told my friend, 'See God has really blessed me!" We went to T. D. Jakes' meeting and we came back. When I got home and tried to sleep, different teams of evil spirits rose up against me. There were teams from Africa, there were two teams from here in the US and they were over 1,000 on each side and they were linked together and coming against me. There were also teams of people who did not like me and they were also out against me. I said to myself, "What in the world is this?" I got up and repented for every-thing that I ever said and did to anyone that was a sin and I reviewed my activities for that day to see where I went wrong in order to repent. I went back to bed and they were all still headed towards me and I said, "Ok Lord, what is the covenant here!" The Lord said, "Remember the MARTA ticket!" You should have seen me at 2 o'clock in the morning looking for the MARTA ticket. Where are you MARTA ticket?

When I found that MARTA ticket, I ripped it into pieces and I went to bed. I renounced every covenant that the ticket represented with the woman because she became the open door against me. Finally, the Lord gave me a vision of her and I said, "In the Name of Jesus, I rebuke the spirit in you that is not of God." I also prayed for her to be delivered from that spirit because if she gives a gift to someone else, she can get the person killed. I am not into gifts because I know that they can become spiritual traps or doors for the devil to afflict a person. This is why the Bible says in **James 1:17** that:

> *17Every good gift and every perfect gift is from above, and cometh down from the Father of lights, with whom is no variableness, neither shadow of turning.*

When it comes to gifts, I'm very leery because if 10 people gave you gifts, if you can find three that are good gifts, you are really doing well. The Lord taught me that a person could only give you what the person has. So, if it is insomnia or cancer that they have, that is what the spirit would try to use them to impart to you. Somebody had given me a purple pair of shoes that matches the exact purple of most of my outfits and I love purple. I liked the shoes and took them home and I was happy about them except for one thing, every morning when I tried to get out of bed it was as if my whole leg had been broken. I could not get out of bed and I said to the Lord, "What is this!" He said to me, "Remember you went and prayed for

169

a lady? What was her condition?" Exactly what was happening to me! And He said, "What did she give you?" A pair of purple shoes! Do you know that all I had to do was take those shoes to the garbage and I never had the problem again? This is why when you begin to get attacked suddenly or develop a condition that is strange, stop and review your recent activities; who you have seen, who you shook hands with, what you bought, who you met and what was given to you so that you can identify where the door was opened for evil spirits to suddenly begin to attack you.

**4. Mental Afflictions:** The devil will also attack you with mental afflictions such as migraines, madness, bipolar, insanity, Alzheimer's, etc. We must not regard them as just medical conditions when we look at them because there are spirits behind them. As I said before, when you come into a place and someone is afflicted with either migraine, bipolar or Alzheimer's, you can know and feel their afflictions. Sometimes you can feel it when they pull into the parking lot! When I am in my house, I can tell when somebody with migraine, Alzheimer's or insanity is coming to visit me as the person is pulling up into my driveway. Every step the person takes towards you makes the person's condition more pronounced. For instance, the spirit of migraine attacks your temples. Bipolar attacks you right above your forehead. Alzheimer's and madness will grab hold of your entire head and make you feel as if somebody is sinking their fingers into your skull and brain. When a person that is afflicted by these spirits walks into a room and takes a seat, I would watch to see the reaction of the people sitting around the person. A lot of times they are trying to straighten their neck and their shoulders. Why? Because there is an emission of oppression from the person sitting next to them and it is coming against them and they do not know it so they begin to rotate their necks and roll their shoulders in an attempt to get some comfort. I usually plead the blood of Jesus around me so that evil spirits do not come from another person to me and when I discern the evil spirit, I would pray for the person carrying the spirit to be delivered. I usually judge such spirits by saying, "You cannot leave this place and go to another place to afflict God's children." I make it a rule to judge every evil spirit that tries to come against me and usually command the evil spirit to go into the abyss and never come back. **I Chronicles 16:22** is my legal ground for judging evil spirits that rise up against me. It says:

*22 ...Touch not mine anointed, and do my prophets no harm.*

**5. Inability to Study the Word or Pray:** We are commanded in **II Timothy 2:15** to study to show ourselves approved unto God.

**15Study to shew thyself approved unto God, a workman that needeth not to be ashamed, rightly dividing the word of truth.**

Therefore when you know that you are not tired or weary but cannot seem to study God's Word or pray

171

for more than 15 minutes without falling asleep, chances are that you are dealing with evil spirits that have been assigned against your prayer and study life. The devil hates to see God's children get into the Word of the Lord to study it or to pray because he knows that the most powerful weapon against him in this entire universe is the Word of God, the Blood and the Name of Jesus. Therefore, he does not want you to pray and he does not want you to develop skills that would be able to root him out. When you know that your diet is proper and you are doing everything you are supposed to and you cannot seem to study or pray without falling asleep, chances are that you are dealing with evil spirits. What you need to do is repent if you or anyone else in your family has ever tried to hinder anybody's prayer life, work life or study life. Ask the Lord to forgive both you and them and to shut the door of the attack so that you can study and pray.

Slumbering spirits (spirits that make people sleepy all the time) are sent to come against your prayer and study life. For example, there was a time my car was in the shop and I took the bus and MARTA while waiting for my car to be fixed. In order to fix my car, the mechanic had to order an engine from Japan and it was going to take four weeks for the engine to arrive. I said, "Devil, for coming against my car, I am going to hit you where it really hurts for these four weeks." I went and ordered a box of tracts and I would get in the bus and train and I would witness on the way to and from work. I told the devil that it was "souls" that I was going to snatch from him. I began to witness to people as if it was going out of business. Before you knew it, I had only been on the bus for about two weeks and most  people knew me on the bus. People would come to me and say, "I've reconciled with my dad since you talked to me, I've gone to the church and I'm now a member of the church." The mother of one little boy said, "You got my son saved last time we saw you on the bus and now on Sundays he insists we all go to church."

On one occasion, I met a lady in the bus and she was alert and talking to another lady when I went to talk to her about Jesus, but as soon as I reached out my hand to give her a Gospel tract, she immediately fell asleep. A spirit knocked her out to sleep right before my eyes and I could not believe my eyes. There was a slumbering spirit that did not want her to hear anything that had to do with Jesus and it knocked her out. I placed the tract in her hand and prayed for her. There are some people that if they even think Bible, weariness and tiredness comes from nowhere upon them. Why? Because the devil is resisting their attempts to strengthen themselves with the Word of the Lord.

**6. Oppression:** This is another way the devil comes against people. The Word of the Lord in **Isaiah 54: 14** says that you shall be far from oppression.

*<sup>14</sup>In righteousness shalt thou be established: thou shalt be far from oppression; for thou*

173

*shalt not fear: and from terror; for it shall*
*not come near thee.*

The devil is a renegade and he likes to oppress people. If you do not know your rights and how to root him out, he can oppress you. He is not a gentle man; he does not get out of your life just because you got born again. You have to run him out like you would a mad dog. When you walk into a place and you begin to feel oppressed in your mind or in your body, I would suggest that you step outside of the place and see if while you are outside you are fine. When you step back into the place and the oppression comes back, chances are you are discerning the oppressive spirits that are in the place. The Lord Jesus had a solution for that. What did He command us to do when we go to a place? He said for us to speak "peace" to the place. Do you know what peace does? When you say "peace be unto a place," because peace is a spirit, it moves around in the place looking for who is worthy for it to rest on. If it cannot find anybody worthy, it comes back to you because there is a scripture that says, "There shall be no peace for the wicked." Therefore when you are about to enter into a place, say, "peace be unto this place." Why? Because the peace you released would go before you to destroy anything that is chaotic in the place. I do not go into anyone's house without speaking peace to the house. I always speak to the house because I want to bless the house and I also do not want to walk into anything that God has not prepared for me.

When you are in an area and you feel a dead weight sitting on you or you are lying down at night and you feel things pressing you, if your Word level is high you will be able to scream "Jesus" or quote scriptures; but if you have not been spending time in the Word of the Lord, then when you are being oppressed by witchcraft spirits at night or early in the morning, you cannot scream because your spirit is anemic. It is not strong enough to fight back. It cannot rise to the occasion. When you have an experience like that, do not feel bad that you could not even scream or move your hand or finger, just get into the Word of God and begin to strengthen your inner man with the Word of God. When you are really feeding your spirit man with the Word of God, it is a mighty warrior in the spirit realm. For instance, my spirit flies in the face of the devil and goes, "Never, Never, Never, Never!"

**7. Suicidal Attempts or Thought:** People who have attempted suicide or have thoughts of suicide are inspired by evil spirits. **Proverbs 11:23** says:

**23The desire of the righteous is only good: but the expectation of the wicked is wrath.**

We have Christians who are having suicidal thoughts. Evil spirits go into their head and get them to look at their past and see how nobody ever cared about them, how their phone has not rang in about a week and how their lives do not really mean anything to anyone. Evil spirits work on their mind. Why?

Because they are trying to get them depressed, discouraged and despair so that they can really feel worthless and when they are in that low place in their lives, then the spirit of suicide comes and tells them, "Oh, this is the time to really end it all. After all, who cares whether or not you are here. Nobody is even going to miss you." People who are weak fall into this lie of evil spirits and they take their own lives and wind up being the "devil's lunch" in hell. The Bible says, "Touch not mine anointed and do my prophets no harm." I tell those who are suicidal that, you do not have a right to touch yourself in a negative way; you do not have a right to kill yourself! I say to those of you who are in the ministry of deliverance that when you are dealing with someone who has suicidal thoughts, do not go after the spirit of suicide alone because before the spirit of suicide comes in, you have the spirit of discouragement, the spirit of despair, the spirit of worthlessness and the spirit of failure. You have all these spirits that lay the groundwork for the spirit of suicide. They work on the person for a long time before the spirit of suicide comes in for the kill. This is why I said before that if you look into the realm of the spirit, you would see that some spirits piggyback on other spirits. There are spirits that are "way-makers" for the main destructive spirit to come in and do the final damage to a soul. Therefore, whenever you are dealing with people that are suicidal, just bear in mind that there are other spirits involved so that you can cover all bases. Do not just pick the fruit, go to the root and find out what is going on so that you can help the person altogether from the beginning to the end.

**8. Family Patterns:** Look at family patterns because **Psalms 112:2** says:

²His seed shall be mighty upon earth: the genera-tion of the  upright shall be blessed.

Also **Psalm 14:5** tells us:

*⁵There were they in great fear: for God is in the generation of the righteous.*

Therefore sicknesses and diseases are not our por-tion. They should not be passed from one generation to another in our family; they are the works of evil spirits. We should not accept them because we are the generation of the righteous; Jesus Christ is our righteousness. Therefore our heritage is the heritage that is void of sicknesses and diseases. Do not let anyone tell you that such and such sickness or dis-ease run in your family. For instance, when you look at some families, you find that the men tend to die when they reach a certain age and the women come down with some kind of disease or sickness at a cer-tain age. These are generational patterns of evil spir-its' afflictions and activities in a family and we must reject the patterns in our generation. We must say no to all evil patterns that we see in our families and con-fess the blessing of the Lord upon our lives. When you are ministering deliverance to someone, talk to them and see about their family pattern because you might be dealing with a generational curse. It might not be as a result of something the person did, parse. It might be something that was passed on to them, so go to the root cause of their problem so that you can effectively minister deliverance to them. Let the person know what he or she needs to repent of. Ask the Holy Spirit for the "Genesis" (root cause) of this curse against the person's family. I once asked the Lord about why the men in a certain family tend to die young and He showed me that an ancestor in that family had starved some women and their children to death during a war and that ancestor brought a curse on his lineage. Whenever any male in that family got to the age of the ancestor at the time the ancestor committed the atrocity, the male became an open target for the devil to come against because of the generational sin. Therefore, a man in that family needs to rise up and repent of the generational sin so that they do not all become victims of the spirit of premature death.

**9. Seeing Evil Spirits/Discernment:** Another way you can identify evil spirits is by seeing them. In **Ephesians 1:18**, God tells us that He wants our spiritual eyes of understanding to be enlightened. This is what Paul prayed over the Ephesians' church.

> *[18]The eyes of your understanding being enlightened; that ye may know what is the hope of his calling, and what the riches of the glory of his inheritance in the saints*

Paul prayed the will of the Lord for the church— that our spiritual eyes of understanding be enlightened. By the power of Holy Spirit, we can see if there are demons in a place, if there are demons in a person or if there are demons in something. As I said before, when I am on the highway driving, if someone that has cancer or some other disease drives by my car, I can tell because each demon has its own foul smell, its own tactic etc. The Lord also told us that the eye is the window to the soul. I can usually see the spirit that is in a person by looking at their eyes. We see this in **Luke 11:34:**

*34 <u>The light of the body is the eye</u>: therefore when thine eye is single, thy whole body also is full of light; but when thine eye is evil, thy body also is full of darkness.*

I believe that the eye is truly the window to the soul. This is why when we are training people for prophetic ministry, we tell them to look at the eyes of the person that they are giving the Word of the Lord. We encourage them not to prophesy over anyone with their eyes closed because they want to see the spirit of the person they are ministering to. If it is the Spirit of the Lord, you will see it and if it is not the Spirit of the Lord, you will see it also because we have radar eyes by the Holy Ghost so you can discern spirits. There are people that I look at and I see that they have a revolving camera lens in their eyes. Their eyes record things for the devil and as a result, demons attack whatever you show them. If you are doing something important and you speak to such a person or show the person what you are doing, that thing will get attacked. That is why we cannot speak our plans to just anyone because some people record for the devil. The devil is not all knowing but he has a networking of evil spirits that sends reports to him. They have a hierarchy through which they file reports and they use people as their agents Whatever the spirit in the agents report as something that would bring about progress or prosperity, the thing would be attacked by the demons.

I remember one time I had a cable antenna that was very good and powerful. With this antenna, you do not really need to get the cable network stations. Someone came to my apartment and remarked about how clear my TV stations were and I told the person that all that I had was the antenna and I showed it to them. We also talked about my telephone line. Do you know that I had lived in that apartment for four years and I had never one day seen a rat? I woke up the next morning and a rat came from nowhere and ate the cable cord to the antenna! It just ate it up and it also ate the telephone cord. When I saw what happened, I knew that a demon was behind it because those were the two things I showed that person. I looked for that rat but I never saw it. It did not touch anything else but the cable and the telephone cords. So, there are some people that record things for the devil to attack.

**10. Words From People's Mouth:** Also, the words

that come out of your mouth can set in order things that will work for your good or things that will work against you. The Lord says in **Matthew 7:20:**

[20]Wherefore by their fruits ye shall know them.

We also learned in **Proverbs 18: 2**1 that:

*21 <u>Death and life are in the power of the</u> <u>tongue</u>: and they that love it shall eat the fruit thereof.*

An individual's words will usually give you a very good idea as to the type of spirit that is in them. For example, the words of someone who carries the spirit of profanity will be quite profane. On the other hand, someone who carries the Holy Spirit will be very quick to bless you and to speak the Word of the Lord over you because by the words you can identify the type of spirit that you are dealing with. Pay attention to people when they are talking. There are some people that when they open their mouth, it is just the devil talking.

**11. Poverty, Unemployment, Homelessness, Destitution, Unexplainable Losses, Divorce, etc.:** When you see patterns of poverty, unemployment, homelessness, destitution, unexplainable losses, single-parent homes in a particular family, know that there are evil spirits assigned against the family or against the people to produce all these adverse conditions. Therefore, when you are ministering to them or if

181

you see that in your own family, either you or them should be quick to repent of whatever sin opened the door for those spirits. Repentance removes the devil's legal grounds to afflict a person.

**John 10:10** tells us that:

> *The thief cometh not, but for to steal, and to kill, and to destroy.*

Do not let the devil steal from you and keep you poor or unemployed and do nothing about it. God wants you to prosper and be in health. God told us His will for us in **3 John 2:**

> *Beloved, I wish above all things that thou mayest prosper and be in health, even as thy soul prospereth.*

Only the devil and his evil spirits do not want us to prosper. This is why we must discern them in order to cast them out.

All these are ways that you can identify the activities of evil spirits. The list is by no means exhaustive. I want you to use it as a guideline to examine your own life in order to see areas where evil spirits have been operating unchallenged. Look at patterns, look at your mother, look at your father, look at your brothers/sisters and your uncles/aunts and see if you are seeing things in your generation that the previous generations also warred against so you can stop the demonic activities. Where there is no repentance there cannot be remission of sin. When you see a pattern, the first thing you do is say, "I don't know what it is Lord, but whatever sin has been committed that is bringing this affliction, I repent right now and I ask that you forgive us." You saw what Daniel said when he was praying for his people in Babylon. He just covered the rebellious sin of the entire nation because he could not possibly know everything that everyone in Israel had done so he just prayed for the entire nation and God sent the angel Gabriel to him in response to his prayer. I said all of these in order to give you a guideline to really look into your own life, look into activities that you see and begin to learn how to identify patterns and begin to see how evil spirits operate.

I am going to address some questions from students and I want you to listen. People will share any spiritual encounter with any spirit; anything that has happened spiritually that they feel is the work of evil spirits. Pay attention to see the activities of each spirit and note how the spirit operates. Remember when I was telling you about the spirit of obesity that was expanding and contracting in a person. At first I did not know what it was but the Lord helped me out when I encountered the spirit the second time around. Sometimes, it takes a few encounters with a spirit before you can effectively identify it.

# Questions and Answers

**_Question #1:_** *I believe in the Lord Jesus Christ and if I pass somebody something and they're evil would that help them any? Like they can give us something and it comes on us but if we give them something can it come on them?*

**_Mary's Answer:_** Remember, I told you to be quick to bless. To be quick to give something to people because you can only give somebody what you have— give them a blessing. There are some people you give something to and that thing becomes the point of blessing in their lives. What you have touched and given to unbelievers will be a blessing in their home unless the Lord tells you not to give them anything. I remember when I visited England the last time, I was going to send someone in the US a postcard and the Lord told me not to send a postcard to the person because there was a spirit of sorcery at work in her home. The Lord told me that the person would put the post card in the living room and the spirit of sorcery in her home would begin to use my handwriting to attack me. This was how the Lord began to teach me about how the spirit of sorcery works. He had to teach me how to give gifts and how to receive gifts. The spirit of sorcery works with physical items and it also works with handwriting. This is why you have to be careful when somebody writes you a letter or sends you a card. When you receive a letter or card from someone who carries the spirit of sorcery and you open the letter and leave it on your table and go to bed, you will find out that you cannot sleep because the spirit of sorcery would be trying to write in your mind and it will keep writing and writing. The reason for this is because your mind was open to it when you read the letter or card! This vexes your spirit and makes you unable to sleep. When I give something to someone I always give it in the Name of the Lord Jesus. I give and receive gifts in the Name of the Lord Jesus and I always bless the person. The Name of the Lord Jesus sanctifies. When you give something to someone in the name of Jesus, it releases a blessing on him or her and by the same token when they give you something, you should received it in the Name of the Lord Jesus Christ. You should thank them for it and ask the Lord Jesus to bless them for it. Right there and then, you have sanctified the gift and whatever the devil was planning to do with it, you have also destroyed. If you know people that carry evil spirits, you always have to deal with them in the name of Jesus when it comes to gifts, some of them might be members of your family. You have to be careful how you handle them so that you do not offend them but at the same time, you sanctify their gifts with the name of Jesus. The Bible says, "<u>All good gifts and all perfect gifts come from above.</u>" This means there are gifts that are not good for you.

***Question #2:*** *A couple of weeks ago, I went and*

185

*stayed with my mother-in-law. A year ago my father-in-law died. My mother-in-law has put a very large picture in the living room above the fireplace. A couple of weeks ago, I went and stayed with her because she was having some health problems. During the night, it started around 12 or 1 o'clock, I kept waking up and I couldn't sleep and it was just like all kinds of activity in my room and I prayed and prayed all night and it happened continuously until 6 o'clock the next morning. I have to go to her house very often. What was revealed to me in the spirit was that she has lifted the picture up as an idol. What can I do when I go over there? I want to sleep.*

**_Mary's Answer:_ It is a question that you ask if you are spiritually sensitive. Yes, some people make their spouse the idol in their lives and all you can do in that regard is pray for her to see the truth. As far as visiting people is concerned, I am very picky about where I go to spend the night. Before I go into a home, I usually speak peace to the house and then bind the strongman in the house and I also bless the house. When I spend the night in a house, it is amazing how the demons in the whole lineage from the person's father's family, the mother's family get very nervous. They immediately feel threatened because they do not know what I am going to do in that family. Therefore, I usually ask permission from the person to cast out any spirit that is not of God that I see. I do not want people to use my discernment gift as a reason to bring me to their home as**

**their spiritual guru, so I make it a rule not to sleep in people's home if I can help it.**

Usually I first recognize that the person has jurisdiction over his or her house but I take authority over my assigned space. You probably can't do that because your mother-in-law is probably not where you are spiritually. And so what I do is ask,

*"Which room have you given me to sleep in?"*

<u>**When you go to a place and they give you a particular space, you have jurisdiction over that space because their giving it to you is a covenant.**</u> **It is yours for the period of time you are there. Therefore, every other thing has to bow in that room**

**.**

**When I am assigned my room in a person's house, the room becomes my legal territory for the period that I am there and I would say:**

"Father, in the Name of the Lord Jesus, I thank you that this room has been given to me for the period of time that I am here. Whatever evil covenant has been made in this house and with this room, I do not partake of it. Therefore, I ask that you sanctify this room so that no evil spirit can come into it for the period of time that I am here and I seal this room with the blood of Jesus. I build a hedge of protection round about the room with the Blood of Jesus."

187

I also speak to the devils and say:

"Whatever covenant was made with you in this house, that is between you and the owner of the house but they have given me this room for this period of time and I have jurisdiction over it. Right now you cannot come in here and you cannot try to make contact with me. I do not like you. I hate you with the perfect hatred, so you have to go from this room. Also, when I leave this room and walk into another room, you must bow and be silent when I come in."

**You can quarantine that room with the Blood of Jesus and make that your domain and when you go to sleep commit your spirit, body, mind and your sleep into the hands of the Lord. I usually ask the Lord to put me to sleep and wake me up at 6 o'clock. That way whatever evil happens in the home cannot come near you because you are covered by the blood of Jesus. That is their home and they have the right to keep their demons if that's what they choose; but those demons do not have the right to touch you. So when I go to someone's house I always ask where have you assigned me and once they give me the place, the first thing I do is take authority over the space. That is what you need to do and put the cross between you and her. The scripture says that the evil bow before the good; the wicked shall bow at the feet of the righteous. You have to let the spirit know that you know your rights because if they think you do not know your spiritual rights, they are going to try to**

**overstep their jurisdiction in order to afflict you.**

*Proverbs 14:19* **says***:*

> *The evil bow before the good; and the wicked at the gates of the righteous.*

*Question #2 Cont'd (Student):* *I sleep in his bedroom though.*

*Mary's Answer:* **That is ok. Still, you do not have to be afraid because you are the one that has the authority even though it is his bedroom. A man's right and authority on earth terminates when the man dies. A person needs a physical body to have authority on the earth. Because he is dead, he does not have any more authority here on earth. He cannot come into that home. He is awaiting judgment. You have a covenant with his Son through marriage, right? So what I would do, because usually when you are married to someone, you married the person and by the virtue of that marriage you have a covenant with his or her mother and father. What you do is bring the marriage covenant you have with the son under the Blood of Jesus and ask the Lord to be the foundation of that marriage covenant. Declare that and you do not partake of any covenant that was made contrary to God's will by the parents and terminate that covenant that is not of God from your marriage. Declare that you do not receive whatever God has not given you from that family.**

That way you can sanctify the foundation of your marriage and you will not have things coming to you through your in-laws. Although I live here in America, I always put the cross between me and my father's family and my mother's family in Africa. Most members of my father's family are Muslims so I make sure that their activities do not impact my life.

*Question #3:* *I'm a prayer warrior but I've been under attack because in my home things just disappear. I remember one day, I was at my wash sink and I had a sweater, an inner sweater and an outer sweater and then I got to the wash sink and all of a sudden it disappeared. I live with my husband and children. We just moved here to Georgia 2-1/2 years ago. That happened on another day. I was in my daughter's house and I took off an underwear and I put on the wash sink and I just went into her bedroom and when I came back it was gone. I could never find it. I asked her and we searched everywhere but you see that spirit is following me and I have to break it.*

*Mary's Answer*: That has happened to me. The first time it happened to me I thought it was really, really strange. Somebody left something for me to give to someone else the next day. I did not want to forget it so I went out and I put it on the passenger's side of my car. I lived alone and I was the only one that has the key to my car and also the only one that drove my car. When I came out in the morning, it was gone. I knew something

**strange had happened and I could not explain it nor did I understand it. I just chucked it up as one of those strange happenings and I moved on with my life.**

Let me balance the strange occurrence out by telling you that strange occurrences also happen on the good side. Some time ago, I got someone to pray a prayer of agreement with me because I needed some finances and I had a specific amount that I needed. I was working in the Children's Ministry and there was a lady that came in and we held hands and we agreed over this yellow piece of paper in which I had itemized everything that I needed and had put a total amount and I said, "Lord this is what I need." As we held hands, we called each item by the amount and we agreed and we prayed over it. Well, it happened that at the church, there was a prayer request table in the sanctuary where people went and placed their prayer request and during service they would pray over them. As soon as I left the lady after our prayer of agreement, I thought, "Let me go make a photo copy of my prayer request on the paper and put it on the table at the alter." I placed the paper in my Bible and went to the copy machine in the next room to make a copy of it. I did not stop anywhere but when I got to the copy machine, the paper was gone! I went back and there was no paper on the ground and it was only the lady and I that were in the children's church. I asked her if she saw the piece of paper we were just praying over and she said no so I headed back to the copy room. I knew something was wrong and as I

191

stood at the copy machine trying to figure out what had happened, I caught a glimpse of the Lord on this throne in heaven laughing. I noticed that He had the piece of paper in His hands and He was smiling. He said to me, "That is one of the most beautiful prayers of agreement that I have seen and you were about to mess it up by walking in unbelief to place the piece of paper again on the table at the alter after you have agreed on every need so I had to stop you from messing up that beautiful prayer of agreement." He had it! That was the good side of it; but then when this other thing was missing in the car, I was like, "Oh my God. Where did the thing go?" I never found it to this day. I knew that the spirit in one of my neighbors took. It took it. I said to the Lord, "Lord what is it?"

This was before I began to learn about the activities of the spirits of sorcery. Sorcery works with items. This is why it is good that you are in America. If you were in Africa and your underwear disappeared, then you would really have to pray because when they take it over there, they want to use it for something very, very evil because your underwear has made contact with your body in an intimate way. In this case, we are going to pray in order to break the assignment of the spirit of sorcery that has been sent against you. There are some people whose lineage goes back to full time paid sorcerers. Maybe down the road in their family history, one of their ancestors made a living as an active sorcerer. Here you are trying to work with Jesus and every once in a while, that spirit of sorcery lets you know that it is in your lineage. Every once in a while, the spirit comes to contend with you.

### *Mary Asks:*
Where are you from originally? Saint Vincent? Ok. It goes beyond your mom and her parents and her parents' parents. Your roots go back to Africa. You don't know who did what.

### *Student's reply:*
*I know my auntie, when I was living in Trinidad, she would come and she would have those shakers and she would be burning incense and stuff and she would turn it over to me and stuff like that. Those are the things I encountered with her.*

### *Mary's Answer Cont'd:* We are going to pray because we do not know exactly how that door got opened. If it is something that is deeper than what you explained, the Lord will reveal it to you. We are going to ask him to forgive you for the particular incidents with your aunt.

### *Question #3 Cont'd (Student):* *Also, I worked at a job as a manager of a supermarket and my boss could not do too much reading and he was dealing with a demonic spirit and he handed me the book to type and I actually left the job because as a child of God I couldn't type the book. Sometimes, I wonder if it is because of that. You know that's a devil spirit.*

### *Mary's Answer Cont'd:* Talking about books,

you can get afflicted by reading a book. Somebody gave me a book written by a 33$^{rd}$ Degree Freemason. It is a book that I want to bring to the awareness of the Body of Christ so I took the book in order to get permission to republish it. After reading parts of that book, for two weeks, I did not know if I was coming or going because of the affliction that I unknowingly opened myself to. I knew I couldn't give the book to the people of God because it would open them up for affliction. I asked the Lord, "Why am I being afflicted by the spirits behind this book?" He said, "Because every confession in that book is in the first person. So when you are reading a book in the first person, you are internalizing what they are saying." I said to myself, until I figure out how I can deal with this book in the third person, I will not give it to another person to read. I took it away from my house because when it is in the house I cannot sleep. The book is such a vital book because it exposes the secrets of the Freemasonry. But, I have to find a way to type and rewrite the book without being afflicted. I figure the Lord is going to help me out with it so I went and put it in a safety deposit box away from my house. When the Lord is ready to deal with the subject using me, He will help me to rewrite the book in such a way that the Body of Christ can know the truth about the activities of the Freemasons without having to internalize their confessions and get afflicted.

## *Mary Prays for student:*

*"Father, in the Name of the Lord Jesus, we thank you for your daughter. We thank you that every plan of the spirit of sorcery against her shall not stand, it shall not come to pass. Father even those things that have been taken from her. Father in the Name of our Lord Jesus Christ, we now put the cross of Jesus between her and those things. Father, any spirit that will seek to use those things as a point of contact to reach her, let the Fire of the Holy Ghost destroy that spirit right now. In the Name of Jesus, we build a hedge of protection round about her and I speak to you spirits of sorcery, I command your assignment to perish right now. Loose her and let her go in Jesus Name. And, Father, we thank you that even as she repents for the sin of sorcery in her family, Father we thank you for answering because you said that with our mouth confession is made unto salvation."*

## *Repeat after me:*

*"Say, Father God, in the Name of the Lord Jesus, I repent of the sin of sorcery for my father's family and my mother's family. Every covenant that we made with the spirit of sorcery, I declare today that it is an abomination. It's a sin against you. Father, I repent of it and I ask that you forgive us in the Name of Jesus. Where we have been walking under curses because of this covenant, Father I ask that you release your blessing upon me, upon my father's family, and my mother's family to destroy all the evil that was sent against us, in Jesus Name. And Father, every item I have lost, I put the cross of Jesus between me and*

195

*those items and I ask that you find them and help me to destroy them so that they cannot be used against me in Jesus' Name. Father, today, in the Name of the Lord Jesus, I judge the spirit of sorcery that was sent against me because it disobeyed your Word that said, "Touch not mine anointed and do my prophets no harm." Therefore, satan, in the Name of the Lord Jesus, I bind you, I rebuke you and I command your activities against me through the spirit of sorcery to perish right now. I send the Fire of the Holy Ghost to burn you and your effects out of our lives in the Name of Jesus. Bow and get out from my life, from my children's life and from my family in Jesus' Name. Father, I thank You and I ask You now for the anointing that destroys the spirit of sorcery. Let it fill me up and overflow in me and use me to deliver other people from this same spirit, in Jesus' Name. I shall go forth as a vessel no longer the victim but a victor in the Name of Jesus. Be destructive to the devil in Jesus' Name. Amen."*

***Question #4:*** *I just wanted to share a dream. I had a dream that I was in a church and I was before people. As I was in that church all of a sudden I looked down and I was totally naked. It seemed like all my clothes had just disappeared off me. I just didn't know the full meaning of that dream.*

***Mary's Answer:*** **Do you remember the books on Visions and Dreams and the Chapter on** *The Sources of Your Visions and Dreams?* **We are going to start back on the teaching series on visions and**

dreams next month. **The devil comes and he tells you that you are naked, that you are not protected but know that you are covered by the Blood of Jesus. The devil's confession is always contrary to the Word of God so when he gives me this type of dream, I go back to** <u>Genesis 1:11</u> **where God said to Adam, "Who told thee that thou wast naked?" So I say to you, "Who told you that you're naked?" You are going to reject the dream by proclaiming that you were not the person in that dream. That was a familiar spirit. It was not really you until you said it was you but the devil is trying to tell you that you are an open (unprotected) target. That is what nakedness speaks of in this dream. When you are not protected or covered, it means you are naked but you know that the Lord is your covering. Therefore, you are not naked. This is why the book of** <u>Proverbs 29:18</u> **says, "Where there is no vision, the people perish—they are naked, lack restraints and protection. So when the devil tells you in a dream that you are walking around in your underwear, cancel the dream when you wake up in the morning.**

<u>Repeat after me</u>:
"Father, I thank you that the familiar spirit in that dream is not me. I know that it is not me because I am dead and my life is hid with Christ in God and I am covered by the Blood of Jesus. Therefore, I am not available to be destroyed by the devil through nakedness.

"Say, Father God, in the Name of Jesus, I thank you

that was not me in that dream. I repent for saying that the spirit was me. I renounce the words and I break their power over my life. That spirit was not me because I'm clothed with the Blood of Jesus and I have on the robe of righteousness. I am not naked because my life is hid inside of Christ. Therefore, I send that dream back to the devil and I say, devil, you are the one who is naked. Let that destruction be upon your head, in Jesus' Name. Amen."

***Question #5***:  *I had a situation where I was at a really wonderful place down at Pastor Henry Wright's. I was almost there for a week. When I returned, I was just really intrigued as to who God would have me run in to and speak to. A certain person came to my door a day after. I was telling him about my experience and he seemed to be enjoying everything I was saying but afterwards, my husband and I were doing fine and we had a wonderful con- versation before we went to bed, everything was just fine. But, in the middle of the night, I knew there was a spirit of fear. I'm not sure it was specifically that spirit but that was the first thing that hit my spirit. And, I said, "you spirit of fear, get out." I did not see anything but I could feel it on my left-hand side. I explained it to my friend and she said, "I think the spirit of fear might have come from him because he's had kind of his arms up about that ministry and also has fear that people are going to go towards the other ministry and not his ministry. My question is, is that possible?*

***Mary asks for clarification:*** *Are you saying that you had a conversation with a person and at night the spirit of fear in the person tried to attack you?*

***Student:*** *Yes.*

***Mary's Answer***: There are some spirits that are called "lingering spirits." There are some people that come into your home and when they leave, the evil spirits in them want to hang around your home long after the people have left your home. You have to drive the spirit away. I usually tell the spirit, you are not welcome in my house and you are not allowed to linger in my home or follow me. Jealousy is one such spirit. When you meet somebody and they hear about what God is doing in your life, if they carry the spirit of jealousy, it might follow you and then next thing you know is that you are being attacked from everywhere. There are some people that while I am standing talking to them, I see them in my closet trying to put on my clothes. In other words, they are coveting the mantle that I have and they want to be the one wearing the mantle instead of me.

There are some people you meet and you have to actually terminate your encounter with them and there are some people who will call your house and you have to terminate the telephone conversation. If not, the spirits in them will continue to speak into your spirit and the result is that you cannot sleep at night. Their spirit would try to change the whole spiritual atmosphere in your house. Yes, the spiritual atmosphere in your house can be affected by their voices because you gave the people permission to speak in your house and the evil spirits in them tries to linger and continue the conversation with you. Never forget that the devil is an opportunist. There was a time I didn't have an answering machine because once I turn off my car in the garage and I'm about to open the door I can tell when someone with an evil spirit has called my house. I can also tell the type of evil spirit that the person carries and I have not even gotten to the answering machine yet. There are times that I do not even play back the message because I do not want to hear the spirit behind the voice that left the message. So, there are lingering spirits that would try to attach to you or your home when you have an encounter with their carrier.

Anger was coming against you from this person as a tool of revenge for what you had done—visiting another ministry. We are going to break that assignment. He was probably just angry with you, but the devil took hold of the anger and tried to use it to attack you in the form of fear.

***Mary***: *Come on over here and let us break it off you.*

Mary Prays for Student:
*"Father, in the Name of the Lord Jesus Christ, I release your daughter from that spirit of anger that was sent against her. I say that the earth is yours and the fullness thereof. Therefore, she shall go to the*

*places that you lead her in Jesus' Name and no one person shall lay claim to her contrary to your will, in Jesus Name. Now, I command the assignment of fear to be destroyed from you. You spirit of anger, go back to the devil in Jesus' Name. Father, we forgive the person and we ask that you forgive him but we speak destruction to the spirit of anger and fear. Anger and fear, we judge you right now in Jesus' Name for it is written, "Touch not my anointed and do my prophets no harm." I rebuke you **and** turn you back to where you came from in Jesus' Name. Blessings be upon you my sister. Amen"*

**Question #6**: *I had a conversation with my mother. My mother and her brother have not spoken to each other for years. They are older now. Now I find out that my brother has the same anger—a generational anger and we have not talked in five or six years.*

**Mary's Answer:** **That is a generational pattern right there. Did your mother have the same problem with her other siblings? It is possible that her dad did same thing with somebody in the family also. We are going to ask the Lord to forgive you but first of all, you are going to forgive them.**

Repeat after me:
"Say, Father God, in the Name of the Lord Jesus, I forgive my brother, my mother and my mother's parents and any other person in my family that has walked in anger towards their siblings and Father, I ask that you to forgive me in every way that I have

judged them by watching them and what they were doing to themselves. I ask that you forgive me and I forgive them in the Name of Jesus. Father, I ask that you forgive us all for going to bed in anger, contrary to Your will. I forgive all the root causes of this anger and I bless all my family members and I ask that you bless them. Let them bless one another in the Name of Jesus. Every covenant that was made with this spirit through our generations, I now renounce the covenant and I say to you anger, I hate you with a perfect hatred. I renounce every covenant with you and I command you to get out because I choose love. I choose to love and I speak love over every person in my family that has been walking in anger. Father, let your love overtake them, let it repair the damage that anger has done and I speak a blessing over me, over my family and I say no more anger in the Name of Jesus. Amen."

***Question #7***: *It was like the lady before me, had talked about... I put down several things in my house and I haven't been able to find them. It's like me and my husband, we've torn the house up looking for certain articles and I cannot find them.*

***Mary's Answer:*** **It is not strange. If it were in Africa you would have cause to be concerned. Although anything the devil does is bad, the level of witchcraft in America is not that sophisticated in comparison to Africa. Did you pray when we were praying with that lady?**

202

<u>Repeat after me</u>:

*"Say, Father God, in the Name of the Lord Jesus, I come before you on behalf of my family and I repent of the spirit of sorcery. I renounce every covenant that we made with the spirit of sorcery by offering items to it and taking items from people and doing evil things with the items and I ask that you forgive us and I ask that you destroy the assignment that was sent against me by that* **spirit. I forgive every member of my father's family, my mother's family that had been involved in** *sorcery. I renounce the covenant they made with the spirit. I declare that the only covenant in my life is the everlasting covenant established by the Blood of Jesus. Therefore, I say to the covenant of sorcery, I do not partake of you, I renounce you, I renounce everything you stand for and I command you today, in the Name of Jesus, to be gone from my life, from my family and I command you also to pay back everything that you have stolen from me, in Jesus' Name. Father, I ask that you find the items that were taken from me and destroy them and be a wall of fire between me and the items that they cannot be used as evil or as a way to get to me in Jesus Name."*

## *Mary Prays:*

*"Father, we thank you that you are the hedge of protection Lord Jesus, over her and that every plan of the spirit of sorcery against her is now destroyed. Those items that can no longer be found, Father in Jesus' Name, we thank you that you are the owner of those items now, find them and destroy them and let*

*your blessing be upon her. I command you spirit of sorcery to loose her and in Jesus' Name I break your assignment and your power over her. Henceforth, you shall no more take one thing from her in Jesus Name. You shall pay back seven-fold for what you have already taken and with all the substance in your house in Jesus' Name. We speak a blessing upon you sister. Amen."*

# Chapter 6

# How to Expel Evil Spirits

This is the final Chapter – *How to Expel Evil Spirits.*
I went through the activities of evil spirits in chapter 3 and in chapter 5 I dealt with how to identify evil spirits. Once we have identified an evil spirit, the next question is, what do we do? The Lord Himself gave us a direct answer to this question—cast out evil spirits. **Mark 16:15-17** says:

> *[15]And he said unto them, Go ye into all the world, and preach the gospel to every creature. [16]He that believeth and is baptized shall be saved; but he that believeth not shall be damned. [17]And these signs shall follow them that believe; In my name shall they cast out devils; they shall speak with new tongues;*
> *[18]They shall take up serpents; and if they drink any deadly thing, it shall not hurt them; they shall lay hands on the sick, and they shall recover.*

We are to be bold in casting out evil spirits because the Lord has given us the authority and He is actually the power backing us up so that no evil can harm us as we cast out evil spirits. The only thing we need to do is make sure we are casting out the evil spirits according to the principle of the Word of the God.
I read in the beginning of Chapter 5 the article of the

205

nun who died because some priests and other nuns tried to cast out the demon that was in her and their actions resulted in her death. We do not want to make such fatal mistakes with people's lives. We want to make sure that what we are doing is by the Word of the God and according to how He said to do it.

The following principles are methods for casting out evil spirits. You must follow them in order to be successful in casting out evil spirits and to avoid being an unnecessary casualty or making others casualties. Before I knew any better in the deliverance ministry, a lady had a baby and I went to see her and I did not know about the spiritual principle of praying, calling on the Name of the Lord or things like that before doing anything. I just sprang into action when I heard the lady groaning in pain and I laid my hands on her in order to rebuke whatever was making her to groan in pain and I almost collapsed. As I reached out to touch her, whatever was in her instantly tried to jump on me. The people around ended up praying for me and it was embarrassing. Prior to laying hands on this lady, I considered the lady a mighty prayer warrior that was doing great destruction to the kingdom of darkness. When I asked the Lord why I almost collapsed, He gave me the understanding that I had made an idol out of her. According to the Lord, she and I both sinned because she allowed me to idolize her so when I went to lay hands on her in prayer, the spirit of idolatry attacked me. After the experience, the Lord began to teach me that before I go out there and do things for God, I

206

had better make sure that there are no holes in my armor so that I do not launch out in ignorance and get afflicted by the devil.

The following story illustrates how well meaning Christians can get afflicted when they operate against the devil in ignorance or when they have holes in their spiritual armor. In chapter 5, I talked about the elderly lady who gave me the purple shoes that I had to throw out because of the evil spirit that was attached to them. After what happened to me with the shoes, I did not go to her and tell her that she had unknowingly passed on her ailment to me through her shoes but after the end of service one Sunday, another lady grabbed her and said to her, "I'm going to drive out that spirit in you today. Come on, I want to pray for you." She grabbed me and said, "Mary we need to cast out this thing from this woman." I followed them and the Lord said to me, "Watch this." So I sat down and she said to me, "Aren't you going to pray?" I said to her, "No, I'll watch you." So she went after the spirit and began to command the spirit to come out of the lady. Meanwhile, the Lord showed me a vision about the lady who was praying over the elderly lady. In the vision, her mother was a reigning principality sent to hinder her. Her mother was sitting on a chair, poised to attack her for trying to move towards the ministry of deliverance! Her mother was also her idol and she needed to repent of the sin before trying to cast out devils.

I shared this story with you because I want you to make sure that you are in right standing with the Lord before you launch out against the devil. The Lord used her to show me how some Christians get afflicted out of ignorance and presumption. When someone comes to you to do this or that, first try to find out what it is that you are dealing with. Do not just charge into prayer in ignorance because you may stir up spirits without knowing what you are praying against. There are some sicknesses or diseases that are the result of a person's sin. The person must repent before you can pray for the person and there are some people that are under God's judgment. Therefore, you must hear from the Lord before you do anything. Listen to the people and see if you are dealing with personal sin, generational curses, unforgiveness or God's judgment in a person's life. There has to be repentance before your prayer can be effective. You can fast and pray all you want but there must be repentance before God can move on behalf of the person. If the person had done something wrong or sinned, the person needs to repent. If you pray in such instances without repentance, you might get afflicted especially if the person is not willing to repent.

In order for you to avoid being an unnecessary casualty of war in going against evil spirits, the following are rules for you to live by.

### Rule #1:  You must be born again.
This is the first step in expelling evil spirits in your life and from the lives of those that you know because

until you are a partaker of the blood bought covenant that God established with the Blood of Jesus, you do not have a legal right to rebuke the devil. If you are not born again and you are going against the devil, it is just a question of time before he takes you out. The devil laughs and scorns those who are not covered by the Blood of Jesus and yet try to rebuke him. As a matter of fact, he can even beat them up just as he did to the seven sons of Sceva in **Acts 19:13-17:**

> *[13]Then certain of the vagabond Jews, exorcists, took upon them to call over them which had evil spirits the name of the LORD Jesus, saying, We adjure you by Jesus whom Paul preacheth. [14]And there were seven sons of one Sceva, a Jew, and chief of the priests, which did so. [15]And the evil spirit answered and said, Jesus I know, and Paul I know; but who are ye? [16]And the man in whom the evil spirit was leaped on them, and overcame them, and prevailed against them, so that they fled out of that house naked and wounded. [17]And this was known to all the Jews and Greeks also dwelling at Ephesus; and fear fell on them all, and the name of the Lord Jesus was magnified.*

They were not in right standing with God before they went after the devil so he beat them up. For instance, there was a pastor that lost his church somewhere in Texas and him and his wife moved down to Georgia. I asked them what happened and they said that they had gone downtown in one of the cities in Texas and did some warfare but when they came back, they immediately started having problems in their church and it resulted in a "church split." They packed up their things and came to Georgia. When I was talking to them, the Lord said, "Ask her (the pastor's wife) what is her name." Her name was after a big old idol and it was foolish for her to be going after an idol downtown when she was a walking advertisement for an idol. When the devil came to revenge against them, he destroyed their ministry in that city.

You have to be careful of what you do and you must know who you are in Christ Jesus. Examine your life closely to see: Are you named after an idol? Are you named after an angel? Is your name from a false religion? There are some people that are named after movie stars, cities, countries or their ancestors. There are some females whose names glorify Lucifer and they have at the root of their names—Luc...! There are other females that each time you call them, you are glorifying the idol in Ephesus because they are named Dia...! Some people are named after angels and God does not share His glory with idols, angels or any other entity and He created man for His glory. Therefore, make sure that even your name gives glory to God and not to some other entity. **This is why you have to know who you are and where you are standing before you go out to war against the devil.** You must be for Christ in every area of your life. Let us look at **Matthew 12:30:**

*³⁰He that is not with me is against me; and he that gathereth not with me scattereth abroad.*

We must first acquire the legal rights as children of God whose sins and rebellion have been washed away by the Blood of Jesus before we can attempt to cast out rebellious spirits. Anyone who is not born again is yet under rebellion against God because of the Adamic sin nature in them. Because of their Adamic sin and nature, they are still very much in the devil's sphere of influence and as a result, have no legal right to rebuke the devil or to cast him out. Only the person who is in obedience or justified (made righteous by the Blood of Jesus) can pull down rebellion. A rebellious person cannot cast out a rebellious spirit. There is a popular saying that two wrongs do not make a right and it is also true in the realm of the spirit. That is why the Bible says, when you have fulfilled your obedience, then you can revenge all disobedience in **II Corinthians 10:6**:

*⁶And having in a readiness to revenge all disobedience, when your obedience is fulfilled.*

If you wonder why God has not dealt with the demon spirits and destroyed them, it is because He has set a time for their judgment and destruction. We as the children of the Living God will judge them because when the devil preached blasphemy and rebellion against God to them, they believed him. They sided

211

with the devil in his attempt to set up his kingdom and be their god. God judged them and cast them down. Now our job is to display the manifold wisdom of God to these principalities and let them know that it is possible to resist the devil, which is something they did not do. **Ephesians 3:9-12:**

> *⁹And to make all men see what is the fellowship of the mystery, which from the beginning of the world hath been hid in God, who created all things by Jesus Christ: ¹⁰<u>To the intent that now unto the principalities and powers in heavenly places might be known by the church the manifold wisdom of God</u>, ¹¹According to the eternal purpose which he purposed in Christ Jesus our Lord: ¹²In whom we have boldness and access with confidence by the faith of him.*

At the end of time, we are going to judge the demons that we are contending with today but right now, as we are working in obedience, we are teaching every entity including the angels in the spirit realm that yes, you can resist the devil and obey God.

## *Rule #2: You need to remove the devil's legal ground against you.*

The next thing you need to do is, remove the devil's legal grounds against you. You saw that in action when we prayed for people that the devil had legal grounds to come against and even take items away from physically because somebody invited the devil into their family. The devil is not a gentleman. He does not say, "Oh, your grandfather invited me into your family but now that you are born again, I really do not think you and I can hang out together." No, the devil goes like, "No, you were given to me and I want you back." Therefore, it is your job to tell him that you are born again now and cast him out. When you know that you're born again and yet, there are things in your life that seem to be generational curses from your ancestors and from where you have been, ask the Lord to reveal the root or legal ground to you. If you have prayed and confessed every scripture you know and nothing seems to change, the next thing to remember is that there might be a legal covenant with the devil somewhere in your family. It tells you that there is a covenant that has been made on your behalf and if you could see the devil in the spirit, you would see him laughing at you as you are trying to get rid of him. He does not give up until you cast him out. You have to ask the Lord to reveal to you the "legalities" and the "technicalities" that the devil is using against you and members of your family. If you do not know the particular covenant, I would say, if it is insomnia for instance,

"I repent of every covenant with the spirit of insomnia. If anyone in my family ever deprived someone of their sleep or told someone they would never sleep in their life, I repent of it and I ask You to forgive me in the Name of Jesus."
I would then rebuke the spirit of insomnia and command it to go."

Always ask the Lord to show you the legal ground that the devil is using to resist your commands. For example, if you know that members of your family have been involved in Freemasonry, the occult, false religion, New Age activities, belief in evolution and other things of such nature, repent because those are legal grounds through which the enemy can attack and resist you. After you have repented, then:

• **Ask the Lord to become Lord of the area of your life that was under attack**
• **Give the area of your life to the Lord**

The Word of God says that when you confess with your mouth the Lord Jesus, you shall be saved if you believe in your heart (**Romans 10:9**).

⁹That if thou shalt confess with thy mouth the Lord Jesus, and shalt believe in thine heart that God hath raised him from the dead, thou shalt be saved.

Make the Lord Jesus Lord of your life in every area of your life that your ancestors had previously given to the devil and take back the legal ground that the devil has against you so that he will no longer have the authority and the ability to contend with you.

### Rule #3: You must know the Word of God.
When we got born again, we became sons and daughters of God vested with all of heaven's authority and power to exercise dominion on earth. We were also

made kings and priests unto God at our new birth. But, **Galatians 4:1-2** tells us:

> *¹ ...That the heir, as long as he is a child, differeth nothing from a servant, though he be lord of all; ²But is under tutors and governors until the time appointed of the father.*

This is one of the reasons why I teach on how to discern and expel evil spirits because we do not want to remain babes. According to scriptures, babes are "unskilled in the Word of righteous" because they are still using milk. They are those that would say to you, tell me what I want to hear, do not tell me that demons exist because I do not want to deal with that. Not only are they childish in their attitude, they are also not ready to walk in the ministry of the Lord Jesus because the ministry of the Lord Jesus Christ is a bold ministry. He spoke to death and death lost its grip on its victims and they came back to life. He spoke to the wind and it became still. His ministry is not for those that want to remain babes but for those that are willing to have their senses exercised to discern between good and evil. The Holy Ghost is now our teacher and He will teach us through pastors, teachers, evangelists, apostles and prophets and as we spend time with Him individually, He will give us personal revelation as to who Jesus is and who we are in Him. As we understand who we are, He also reveals to us the extent of the authority that God has invested in us. It is the Holy Spirit that teaches us

215

how to use our God-given authority. I say to you that the devil is not afraid of any human being who does not know the Word of God because the #1 weapon that he fears is the Word of God. If you look at **Matthew 4:3-11**, you will see what the Lord Jesus did when the devil came against him. He used the Word of God as His weapon!

> *³And when the tempter (the devil) came to him, he said, If thou be the Son of God, command that these stones be made bread. ⁴But he (Jesus) answered and said, It is written, Man shall not live by bread alone, but by every word that proceedeth out of the mouth of God. ⁵Then the devil taketh him up into the holy city, and setteth him on a pinnacle of the temple, ⁶And saith unto him, If thou be the Son of God, cast thyself down: for it is written, He shall give his angels charge concerning thee: and in their hands they shall bear thee up, lest at any time thou dash thy foot against a stone. ⁷Jesus said unto him, It is written again, Thou shalt not tempt the Lord thy God. ⁸Again, the devil taketh him up into an exceeding high mountain, and sheweth him all the kingdoms of the world, and the glory of them; ⁹And saith unto him, All these things will I give thee, if thou wilt fall down and worship me. ¹⁰Then saith Jesus unto him, Get thee hence, Satan: for it is written, Thou shalt worship the Lord thy*

216

***God, and him only shalt thou serve. <sup>11</sup>Then the devil leaveth him, and, behold, angels came and ministered unto him.***

As you can see from the above scriptures, the Lord's response to the devil's request each time was, **"It is written."** The devil tempted the Lord with the pride of life by requesting Him to do a spectacular miracle in order to prove that He is the Son of God— command stones to become bread. The devil tempted Him with the glory of all the kingdoms—again he tried to use the pride of life, love of fame and fortune to trap the Lord. The devil tempted the Lord in every key area that he (he the devil) comes against every human being—the pride of life, love of money, love of prestige and idolatry. Again I say to you that the Word of God is what the Lord Jesus quoted against the devil. The devil knew the power of the Word of God for he himself quoted the scripture to the Lord. So you see that the Word of God is very, very powerful. It is the primary weapon that the devil fears. This is why he hates Christians who study the Word of God because he knows that if you go into the Word and you keep on studying, you are going to be exercised and become strong in the things of God. As you wax stronger and stronger, you become a powerful weapon that he has to contend with. Therefore, he tries to nip you in the bud by making sure he distracts you or worries you so that you cannot get into the Word of God. There are some people that are afraid of the Word of God and there are those that have said that the devil threatened to kill them the day they began to study the Word of God. Should the devil ever try to make you afraid or threaten you for reading the Word of God, just remember what the Lord Jesus told us. He said that the devil is a liar and the father of lies. He cannot harm you if you spend time in the Word of God.

### Rule #4: You have to learn to Fast and Pray.

Another powerful weapon against the devil is fasting and praying. The Word of God tells us in **James 5:16** that:

> [16]*Confess your faults one to another, and pray one for another, that ye may be healed.* _The effectual fervent prayer of a righteous man availeth much._

Prayer ushers in the presence of God and the devil cannot abide where God's presence is. Therefore, we cast out devils by just our simple act of praying. For instance, in 1993, someone gave me a T-shirt while I was in the hospital and I did not like the T-shirt because it looked like it had been worn and it had a hole in it but I kept it. At this time, I was not yet aware of the scripture in **James 1:17** that:

> [17]_Every good gift and every perfect gift is from above, and cometh down from the Father of lights_, *with whom is no variableness, neither shadow of turning.*

In 1994, I pulled the T-shirt out and I put it on and

it became the T-shirt that I wore to bed. I began to suffer affliction at night and in my sleep. One evening, I took the T-shirt and I threw it into the corner of the room and I began to praise the Lord. I began to dance around and as I was dancing, the Lord showed me a vision of the demon that was on the T-shirt. It was a female spirit in the form of the lady who gave me the T-shirt. In the vision, every time I spoke the Name of Jesus, I would see the spirit hold her ears because the Name of Jesus pierced her like a knife. When I looked at her on the T-shirt and saw the tormenting effect of my prayer on her, I decided to keep calling on the name of Jesus as I prayed just to torment her some more. When I felt that I had tortured her enough, I took the T-shirt and cut it up and threw it away. This incident allowed me to see the importance of prayer. Prayer allowed me to see the very spirit that had been vexing me at night.

Also, when a father brought a boy that was afflicted by the deaf and dumb spirit to the disciples and the disciples could not cast the devil out, the disciples later wanted to know why they could not cast out the devil and the Lord said to them, **"Howbeit this kind goeth not out but by prayer and fasting** (Matthew 17:21). So when you are praying and fasting, you actually cast out the devils that try to hide or resist your attempt to cast them out; especially what we call "lingering spirits" (spirits that try to linger around you and in you) but as you keep calling on the Name of the Lord Jesus and getting into the presence of the Lord, even the lingering spirits have to leave.

Another time the Lord showed me the effect of prayer and fasting was when I came out of the hospital in 1993. He said to me, "Give me something to work with— pray, read psalms, and let me hear my Word coming out of your mouth." Therefore, I began to read the psalms out loud and to learn how to pray with the psalms. I would read out the psalms out loud to the Lord and I would just confess and put my name in each Psalm that had a promise for the believer. While praying one day, He gave me a vision: God the Father was sitting on the throne and the Lord Jesus was sitting beside Him. I was walking towards them but there was this woman (an evil spirit) that was dressed in a black lace material from head to toe. She held on to my leg as I was trying to move towards God the Father and the Lord Jesus. It was obvious that she did not want me to take any step forward but I was determined to get to the father and the Lord so I dragged her along. I saw God the Father and the Lord Jesus lean forward from their throne to look at what was trying to keep me from going forward. I got stronger as I got closer to them and the grip of the women was losing its strength on me. Finally, right before I made it to where they were sitting, the woman just went limp and died in the presence God the Father and the Lord Jesus. God the Father said, "Oh well." In other words, your problem with her is over! I did not have an enemy to contend with any longer. There are some spirits that cannot abide the presence of God. Later in my Christian walk, I found out who the woman was that had unleashed the death spirit against me. It was shocking when I found out her real life identity.

By making the determination to pray and to praise the Lord, you clear your whole spiritual atmosphere of demonic activities. You would rid your home and yourself of "household wickedness." Household wickedness speaks of spirits that are sent to your family to monitor what you do in the house. They are ease-dropping spirits and Peeping-Tom spirits. Therefore, when you are praying, bind them with the Word of God and the Blood of Jesus. Every time you pray, pray with the Blood of Jesus because you drive demons crazy when you speak the Word of God and mention the name of Jesus.

### Rule #5: Pray with the Name of Jesus.
Another tool you can use to cast out demons is the use of the Name of Jesus. The Lord himself gave us the legal authority and power to cast out unclean spirits or devils in His Name. He said in **Mark 16:17**:

> *[17]And these signs shall follow them that believe; In my name shall they cast out devils; they shall speak with new tongues;*

So, be bold to cast out devils in the name of the Lord Jesus.

And also **John 14:14**:

> *[14]If ye shall ask any thing in my name, I will do it.*

221

The Lord Jesus is the very authority that is backing us when we speak the Word of God and when we use His name. I say to you, that the Name of Jesus is heaven's valid currency. It produces results. We are to use the Name of Jesus to enforce the Kingdom of God on earth so that God's will can be done on earth as it is in heaven. The Lord Jesus is in heaven but we the believers (His body) are on earth. We are to enforce His kingdom rule and dominion here on earth and we are to do it in His Name. All of heaven backs the Name of Jesus. God also commanded every thing in heaven, on earth and under the earth (which is the realm of evil spirits) to bow at the mention of the Name of the Lord Jesus. We see this in **Philippians 2:10-11:**

> *[10]That at the name of Jesus every knee should bow, of things in heaven, and things in earth, and things under the earth; [11]And that every tongue should confess that Jesus Christ is Lord, to the glory of God the Father.*

All heaven's arsenal is ready to punish and destroy any evil spirit that does not obey any command that you issue in the Name of Jesus and in faith. This is why the devils fear any believer who understands his or her legal authority, walks in faith and can pull the Name of Jesus as a sword against them. Not only have we been given authority to use the Name of Jesus, but we have also been given authority over all evil spirits. **Luke 10:19-20** says:

*<sup>19</sup>Behold, I give unto you power to tread on serpents and scorpions, and over all the power of the enemy: and nothing shall by any means hurt you. <sup>20</sup>Notwithstanding in this rejoice not, <u>that the spirits are subject unto you;</u> but rather rejoice, because your names are written in heaven.*

God has made the evil spirits subject unto us. He has given us authority to bind them, to punish them, to tread them down and to root them out. They cannot harm us if we walk according to the commandment that we have been given—**Put on the whole armor of God**. I talked about this in the chapter on Can a Christian Have a Demon? I said a Christian would be free from evil spirits' activities to the extent that a Christian has put on the whole armor of God. You cannot be living like a child of the devil; lying, cursing, stealing, cheating, fornicating, etc., and expect the devil not to have a legal hold on you. You cannot live contrary to the Word of God and say that the devil has no way to get to you. You would be kidding yourself. This is why it is vital to put on the whole armor of God, the helmet of salvation, breastplate of righteousness, belt of truth etc. You are required to do these things in order to keep the demons away from you. You are protected from evil spirits to the extent that you do this. You must purpose to work in peace with everybody. Your feet are supposed to be clothed with the Gospel of peace. Evil spirits will latch on to you if you quarrel with people in the places you go to and they can follow you home.

### *Rule #6: Use* the Blood of Jesus.

Another weapon against the devil and his demons is the Blood of Jesus. I told you before that whenever you mention the Name of the Lord Jesus or the Blood of Jesus, demons tremble. **Revelation 12:11** tells us about the power of the blood of Jesus:

> *[11]And <u>they overcame him by the blood of the Lamb,</u> and by the word of their testimony; and they loved not their lives unto the death.*

The blood of Jesus has power not just to cleanse us of our sins but also to remove evil spirits and their effects from our lives and from our dwelling places. Evil spirits cannot stand the sight of the blood of Jesus because they know that the blood of Jesus has the power to instantly destroy them. This is why they flee whenever the blood of Jesus is invoked against them in faith and with genuine God-given authority.

There are some scholars in the Body of Christ that do not believe that Christians have the right to plead the blood of Jesus. Their argument is that only the High Priest had the right to apply the blood of the lamb in the Old Testament. They believe that since the Lord is the only High Priest, He alone has the right to use His own blood. What these scholars fail to remember is that, yes, the Lord Jesus is now the High Priest before God on our behalf forever but **He lives in us**. We are His body and He is the head of His Body. We

224

are not apart from Him but one with Him. He works in us both to will and to do of His good pleasure— **Philippians 2:13:**

>*¹³For it is God which worketh in you both to will and to do of his good pleasure.*

The Lord works through us as His vessels and when we plead the blood of Jesus, He backs us up. These scholars also forget that God promised protection to the children of Israel who applied the blood of the lamb to the doorposts of their houses – **Exodus 12:13:**

>*¹³And the blood shall be to you for a token upon the houses where ye are: **and when I see the blood, I will pass over you**, and the plague shall not be upon you to destroy you, when I smite the land of Egypt.*

The application of the blood of the lamb by the children of Israel was a type of the power of the blood of Jesus; the true Lamb of God that was to come. **Not all the children of Israel that applied the blood of the lamb to the doorposts of their houses where High Priests.** We who believe in Jesus Christ have been grafted into the "true vine" which is Israel. Therefore, by our spiritual birth—adoption, we are "Jews". We are now part of the tribe of Judah through our Lord Jesus Christ. Therefore, we have the right to apply the blood of Jesus over our lives for protection and over our dwelling places just like the children of Israel did before they left Egypt.

225

Also, when a person is told to appear before a judge in a court of law, the judge would usually ask the person what the person pleads. The person will either plead guilty or not guilty. In the highest court of justice that met before God Almighty, the Lord pleaded **not guilty** on our behalf because He took all the punishment for our sins. **Therefore, when we plead the blood of Jesus, we are announcing to all principalities and powers that God has declared us not guilty. Therefore, they do not have any legal rights to afflict us!** God sends angels to enforce our not guilty status when we plead the blood of Jesus against evil spirits that seek to afflict us.

## Rule #7: *Ministering Angels.*

Another weapon that you can use when you are casting out evil spirits is the ministering of angels. **Psalms 91:11** tells us that God has given his angels charge over us to keep us from harm.

> *[11]For he shall give his angels charge over thee, to keep thee in all thy ways.*

Therefore, we should always speak the Word of God so that His angels can arise and protect us. Also, know that the angels listen to perform the Word of God that we speak in faith. Therefore, speak the Word of God in faith to activate the ministering angels on your behalf—**Psalm 103:20:**

> *[20]Bless the LORD, ye his angels, that excel*

226

*in strength, that do his commandments, hearkening unto the voice of his word.*

Angels listen to hear who is speaking the Word of God in faith so that they can perform it. Therefore, be quick to speak the Word of God in faith. There are scriptures that I speak a lot when I want the Lord to activate His angels on my behalf.

A popular question in Christendom is, "Do we have authority to dispatch angels or do we have to tell God to send angels on our behalf?" I say that the scripture above answers the question for us because it tells us that the angels hearken to the voice of His Word. Therefore, I speak the Word of God that dispatches angels because it is the Word of God that the angels themselves listen to hear in order to go into action. I speak the following scriptures that dispatch warring angels.

**Psalm 35:5-6:**

> *5Let them be as chaff before the wind: and let the angel of the LORD chase them. 6Let their way be dark and slippery: and let the angel of the LORD persecute them.*

Scriptures of this type directly activate the angels because it is not your Word that you are speaking but the Word of God! Hebrews tells us that angels are sent to minister to us.

**Hebrews 1:14:**

>  *[14]Are they not all ministering spirits, <u>sent forth to minister for them who shall be heirs of salvation?</u>*

**Angels have already been <u>sent</u> on our behalf, all we need to do is speak the word that they respond to which is the Word of God!** Remember that the Archangel Michael was sent to help the Angel Gabriel who was fighting on behalf of Daniel. They both fought the Prince of Persia on behalf of Daniel because Daniel had prayed.  He reminded God of His Word that said the children of Israel were only going to be in captivity for 70 years. Therefore, when Daniel read the book and discovered that the 70 had been accomplished, he petitioned God to fulfill his promise.  God had to do something because God is a man of His word. He sent the Angel Gabriel to help the Prophet Daniel.

## *Rule #8: Walk in Righteousness.*

 Also, the Word says to walk in righteousness.  This is what I was telling you when I talked about putting on the whole armor of God, purpose in your heart to think righteously, to speak righteously and to speak the truth in all things.  Let your activities be in line with the Word of God, choose to live in peace with people, choose to avoid strife and walk in faith because it is the shield that repels evil spirits. Finally, you must be skilled in the Word of righteousness. One cannot live one's life in violation of God's spiritual dress code and expect the fiery darts of the devil (evil spirits) not to penetrate ones' mind and body. Those who live in violation of this spiritual dress code can die prematurely of sickness and diseases or leave their lives open for the devil to attack.

Hopefully when you look at the scriptures on putting on the whole armor of God **(Ephesians 6:11-18)**, you should begin to see it in a different light because it is what you are required to do to keep the devil and his evil spirits away from your mind and your body. God saved your spirit but he gave you the responsibility to protect your mind and your body.

### *Rule #9: Walk in Love:*
According to **I Corinthians 13:8**, love is a very powerful weapon and it never fails.

**[8]Charity never faileth.**

Purpose to walk in love. Evil spirits delight in stirring up fights and strife; therefore, they cannot stand acts of love because it is contrary to their nature. They have the nature of the devil. When they willingly submitted themselves to the devil, they totally took on his evil nature and as a result, they cannot stand when you are performing an act of love. This is what Jesus was telling us when He said that when someone slaps you on the right cheek; turn the other cheek to them also. Because evil spirits expects you to fight back when someone wrongs you, they are baffled when you respond in love.

## *Rule #10: Walk in Forgiveness.*

We must also purpose to walk in forgiveness because unforgiveness invites evil spirits. The Lord told us in **Matthew 18:33-35** that anyone who would not forgive would be delivered to tormentors. The tormentors are nothing but evil spirits. Sometimes if you are too stubborn, God would let them have a go at you for a while until you learn that you have to forgive others when they offend you.

> *[33]Shouldest not thou also have had compassion on thy fellow servant, even as I had pity on thee? [34]And his lord was wroth, and delivered him to the tormentors, till he should pay all that was due unto him. [35]So likewise shall my heavenly Father do also unto you, if ye from your hearts forgive not every one his brother their trespasses.*

Unforgiveness is a wide door that attracts evil spirits because they will remind you of what people have done to you and how you should really get even with them. They will give you thoughts such as, "did you see how Kim looked at you? After everything that you have done for her, she still continues to speak against you. She is very ungrateful. You need to really let her know that you are not a push over." Sometimes, the evil spirits would send someone to speak to you in order to stir up trouble. The person might say to you, "I just want to tell you this, I don't know if you have noticed how so and so talks to you? They are rude

to you and you shouldn't have to put up with that."
Evil spirits can use other people to fester a wound
until it becomes something big that provokes you to
react negatively. You can receive your deliverance
when you purpose to forgive everybody that you are
holding in unforgiveness. You can eliminate the legal
grounds that evil spirits are using against you when
you choose to forgive those that have offended you.

### *Rule #11: Make Right Confessions.*
 Some people have a negative confession over themselves and their words are actually the legal grounds
the devil uses to afflict them. Did you ever watch the
TV program called *Sanford and Son?* Remember that
old program? He was always talking about having the
"big one" (heart attack). And how did he die? He had
the "big one" right on the set! You have to be careful of what you say because the scriptures say that,
"Death and life are in the power of the tongue." So do
not speak words of death or words that are evil over
your life and think the devil is just going to let it go by.
He will use your words against you.

   I remember the time that I worked briefly in
a computer firm. It was about my second day in the
office and someone came in with a story about some
lady that had died in her sleep. I was there to relieve
a lady that was going on maternity leave. The lady
that was about to go on maternity leave over heard
the story of the lady that had died in her sleep and
she said, "that is how I want to go." Before she could
finish the sentence, I saw the spirit of death descend

into her cubicle in the workplace! I was standing there thinking, "Some people know how to invite death with their mouth." The next day when she was packing up her things to go on maternity leave, I knew that she was not aware that she had used her mouth to put herself in a place where death could take her out. She expressed the desire for death and devil was going to pick the time to accomplish it. The Lord then reminded me of the vision that He gave me before ever stepping into the company. I immediately realized that the Lord sent me to the office to snatch the lady from the jaws of death. I began to pray for the Lord to give me an opportunity to pray with her. During the three days I had with her, I had the opportunity to go to lunch with her. We talked and I told her about the Lord Jesus and His plan of salvation for us all and she received the Lord as her Savior. I also told her that she needed to cancel something she had said. I tried not to scare her because I did not know her level of understanding of spiritual matters. I told her to never confess that she would want to die in her sleep because if during the time of her delivery she is placed under anesthesia, she might not wake up. I did not share with her that I already knew that the devil was planning to do that to her during her time of delivery. You might wonder why when you pray with people sometimes they still end up dead. One of the reasons is because some of them spoke words of death over their lives during their lifetime and the devil used those words against them whenever their lives were in the balance between life and death. We do not need to arm the devil against us. Therefore, you have to be careful that your words do not unleash evil spirits against you. One of the ways you can also get rid of evil spirits is to make sure your confession is right in line with the Word of God.

During my stay in the hospital in 1993, I went to see the psychiatric doctor. He said he was told that my mind was going round and round in a circle, spinning out of control. I told him that the Lord has given me the spirit of power, love and **a sound mind**. He replied that he was told that my mind was spinning out of control and he drew a circle and then asked me if I was still seeing Jesus as he had been informed? (That was my illness—seeing Jesus!) He asked me, "Do you truly see Jesus?" I told him yes. Every time the doctor asked me if I saw Jesus since the last time we spoke and I said yes, the doctor would increase the dosage of my medication. I was in the hospital diagnosed as irrationally clinging to the Bible. What they did not know was that when a person is in the psychiatric hospital that is when the person really needs a Bible. They were determined to keep me in the hospital until the day that I got rid of my Bible and I was not going to get rid of my Bible for any reason. Throughout the time I was in the hospital, I confessed what God's Word said about me and rejected their evil reports. I knew that my seeing Jesus was not a sickness.

These are the keys on how to expel evil spirits. Study them in-depth because God brought you in contact with this book in order for you to learn not only how to be delivered, but for you to be a vessel He can use to deliver other people. You need to know how to deliver people from evil spirits according to the word of God so that you do not end up becoming a casualty.

# Questions and Answers

***Question #1***: *When I bought my house, one night I was laying in the bed and my mom came in here and she said, "come, come quickly. I want you to see something. You're not going to believe me if you don't come." So I go out to my front porch and there's something balled up on the front porch. It was in a ball. Momma said, "What is that?  It wasn't there when we came in." When she said that, I looked and there was a bird and she went in the kitchen and she got some bleach, some salt and some hot water and she dashed it up there, a head came up and it turned two ways. It was a bat and it almost scared the day-lights out of me.*

***Mary's Answer***: **One of the things I will bring to your attention very quickly is that we need to have a balance with spiritual matters.  There are some things that happen, like if a house is vacant for a while, birds can build nests because animals for some reason can tell when a house is vacant. When that happens, you do not have to spiritual-ize something that is not there because I would not say that it was a spiritual attack because you and your mom got rid of it with bleach.  Not only**

**that, you probably disturbed the bat that was feeling that the empty house was a safe place to build a nest and raise her babies. But if you feel like anything was in there, just plead the blood of Jesus over it.**

**Usually when you buy a house or you move into an area there two things you need to do:**

1. The neighborhood you are moving into—Is it named after a person? When I moved to Lawrenceville, I had to tell the spirit of "Lawrence" (principality), "I do not know what you did to get the city named after you because it is idolatry. I do not know if it was a favor or an honor for some heroic act that you performed but whatever it is, I do not want the covenant that was made with your name in this city. I do not partake of the covenant with you. I reckon it dead on the cross of Jesus. I put the cross between me and you and your activities and whatever it was that was done with you in this city. I'm coming in here with the scripture that says, "The earth is the Lord's and the fullness thereof."

2. The next thing is to sanctify the house and cleanse it from whoever lived in the house before. You need to declare that whatever covenant they made with the house prior to your buying the house is no longer valid. Their jurisdiction ended when they sold the house to you. When they signed the paper, there was a legal contract and you therefore must terminate their rights to the property. Declare your ownership

of the house and plead the blood of Jesus over it. You cannot allow any spirit that is contrary to the spirit of the Lord Jesus to come into the place.

**If you have not done that, just go pray over the place and anoint it with oil. Bless your home always.**

***Question #1 Cont'd***:  *I actually had to do that because one night my mom went to my sister's house and I was lying in the bed and I kept hearing footsteps like somebody was walking up in the attic, you know, like there was a person up there. It was just noise that was trying to frighten me out of the house. One night, I just got up and I said, "Wait a minute devil, I bought this house. This is my house. You are going to get out of here." I just got the oil and started going through the house saying, "I bind you in Jesus' Name. You're getting out of this house. It's my house!" I didn't hear anything else in that house again. My son moved in and he was living in the other bedroom. One day he said, "Momma there's something in your house. I'm lying in bed and I'm hearing stuff in the closet and I get up and open the closet and there's nothing in there." I said to him, "You brought that spirit in here with you." So I just wanted to ask you a question about that...*

***Mary's Answer***:  **How many of you have heard things walking about in your home. In my book: *Unveiling the God-Mother,* I talked about the religious spirits and how they contend with people who have a covenant with them. For instance, if**

you have believed any other doctrine that is contrary to the Bible, when you are praying or you are in the house, the religious spirits will contend with you for the space. Also, if the people that lived in the house before you bought it worshipped a different god, you would have religious spirits contending with you for the property. Therefore, if you are in the house and you hear things moving while you are trying to pray or things suddenly begin to fall off the wall, you should immediately realize that you are dealing with religious spirits. If this is the case, terminate the legal rights of religious spirits by removing the rights of whoever lived in the place before you. Establish your boundaries and your ownership of the property with the Lord Jesus and then speak scriptures that dispatch angels to root out whatsoever is not of God in the property. The devil does not just go away because a Christian moved into a place. He is going to see how far he can push his presence and how much of him you would ignorantly allow in your home. It is your job to cast him out.

*Question #2:* *I repented over a lot of things that I've done in the past and I turned my life over to God but still sometimes I have these dark dreams a lot. And, I'm not participating in anything dark that I've acknowledged so I would like God to a stop because I am tired of it.*

*Mary's Answer:* You're a candidate for the series that begin next month. I am going to start a new teaching series on *Visions and Dreams.* These classes teach you about: The key principles about visions and dreams, Sources of Your Visions and Dreams, How to Identify the Sources of Your Visions and Dreams, How to Analyze the Contents of Your Visions and Dreams and Types of Visions and Dreams. You'll benefits from the teaching but meanwhile, get a copy of my book titled, *Keys To understanding Your Visions and Dreams: A Classroom Approach.* Begin to read it before the next class. If the devil can't get you during day, he'll try to come against you in your sleep through dreams.

*Question #3:* How about if somebody in my family is still going to psychic and stuff?

*Mary's Answer:* You put the cross between you and the person. Then you say, "If they take my name to the psychic, let the Blood of Jesus answer them." The Lord taught me that I am not responsible for other people's actions but I can keep their actions from impacting my life by placing the cross between them and me and by speaking the Word of God and by using the Name and Blood of Jesus. I always put the cross of Jesus between every member of my father's family, my mother's family and me. I even place the cross between me and my father's children, my mother's children and their spouses. I place the cross also between everyone that dislikes me and me and I say, "I hide my name in the thunder of God's voice. Therefore if anyone calls my name for evil, let the thunder from God's voice answer in my place." Therefore, if anyone takes my name to the psychic or witchdoctor, the person would be surprised at what would happen to the person, and the psychic or the witchdoctor. You repel things sent against you by placing the cross of Jesus between you and the things. The scripture says, "Ye are dead and your life is hid with Christ in God." They cannot kill a dead man twice.

***Question #4***: *A long time ago, I think I was about 13 years old when my grandmother took me up to the alter. "Pray, pray, you know how grandmothers do. Anyway, I'm just starting thinking about this again recently. I had broken through the spirit realm and it was like I was before God the Father and the throne room. But, right as I broke through, something tapped me and I turned and it was a female in a black wedding gown. It was the month of August and she had combat boots and gloves on. She had a veil and he had no eyes and I just remember looking at her mouth. She had no face and the demon voice spoke out of her and she was like, "You better stop praying because Jesus is not coming." So I took a swing at her. My uncle came and he said, "What is wrong with you?" because I'm at the front of the church fighting and nobody's there. So, it was like the Holy Ghost rose up in me when that happened. I had no fear, I was just hot and mad but my grandmother told me anytime you break through the spirit realm like that,* *a hindering spirit can come. But recently someone told me that it was a female principality assigned to my family. What do you say?*

**<u>Mary's Answer</u>: I do not know if it was a principality but I do know that she was assigned against you because she was dressed for combat. The thing about it is that you overcame her. I would think that it is now in your past. So stop trying to drag her into the future because you should be seeing her as something that you overcame years ago. Because I have overcome the spirit of death, I do not see myself as someone that is still contending with the spirit of death. I know that I have the victory over death and I walk as someone who treads on the spirit of death by the power and life of Jesus. So, I would think, because you were able to break through and defeat her way back then that you have the victory over her. Do not let the devil bring her back into your future. You should move on. This is why Paul said, "I forget about the things that are behind, I reach forth to the things that are before." You should actually be seeing yourself now as one that has successfully overcome the spirit of death that God can use to deliver people who are afflicted by death instead of still going back trying to seek deliverance from death. This is why the Bible also says, "Ever learning and never coming to an understanding." You should understand what has already been done for you and apprehend it and begin to see yourself as such. Let's pray for you to come into a realiza-**

**tion of what God has done for you:**

## Repeat After me:
*"Father God, in the Name of the Lord Jesus, I thank you that I overcame the spirit of death by the power of the blood of Jesus and I thank You that I am a vessel who treads upon death in Jesus' Name and in the authority of the Word of God and by the Name of Jesus. Therefore, I ask for forgiveness for not fully understanding what you have already done for me. I ask that you release me now to be a vessel that you use to bind, rebuke and root out death. Thanks for using me to pull it down and to destroy it in the Name of Jesus. Amen."*

***Question #5***: *I have a question and a concern. I have a 10-year old nephew and my sister and my brother-in-law allow him to have Pokey Man cards and that type of thing. My concern is, I think there is something going on there. But my question is what can I do? Because I don't have the authority to take the cards away.*

***Mary's Answer:*** **As I stated before, one of the things the Lord taught me some years ago is that I am not responsible for other people's actions. When we all stand before God on the last day, each person will give account of his or her life. Nobody else will come into the equation. It will between them and God and what they did. You are right to be concerned about your nephew because those Pokey Man cards open children up**

241

for demonic attacks.  One of the things that you can do is go to the Lord in prayer and let the Lord do something to remove those cards because you can talk to them until you are blue in the face and they would not believe you that those cards are bad.  But when you, out of love and concern for your nephew, go to the Lord and ask the Lord to forgive them because they do not know what they are doing, then the Lord can move on their behalf. The Lord told me years ago that unbelievers sin, that's what they do—sin!  The way of unbelievers is to sin. God is not shocked by the actions of unbelievers. When you call on the Lord, He can intervene.  The little boy could wake up one day and with the Lord's intervention declare that he does not want the cards anymore and that would be the end of that.  When he grows up and he comes to your house, then you can pray with him to renounce every evil card he ever played with as a child.  Right now, the grace of God covers him.

***Question #6:*** *There are two things or concerns that I have. I'm divorced and my ex was a Freemason. We have two children together and I believe some of the things that he was involved in or is still involved in have affected their lives. They've had a lot of difficulties going through and we moved away from Miami, moved here to Georgia and now he's back in their lives and I can see their lives going down the tube since he's now involved with them.*

My second question is there've been bad marriages

in my family and divorce is very prominent. My parents stayed together until my father died. I don't know where the door was opened but it's still prevalent. I have sisters who are very strong in the Lord but they have very mean husbands and their lives are in torment.

***Mary's Answer*:** Let's take the first one. One of the reasons I wanted to publish a Freemasonry book was because it actually tells you the initiation rites that an initiate (somebody who gets initiated into Freemasonry) is made to go through. What they do during the ritual is that they actually bring the person into a room with a noose on the initiate's neck and the officiating person would hit the initiate and the initiate would fall to the ground. When the initiate gets up, he would confess that it is no longer him that lives but Hiram Abiff that now lives in him. This is called (fake) a death and resurrection experience of the initiate. When a person undergoes this rite of the death and resurrection of the initiate, the person ignorantly sanctifies himself and all his future offspring (the seed he carries in him) to the spirit of Freemasonry, which is none other than the devil himself. The devil is at the head of Freemasonry but the initiate is not told the truth until he graduates to the degree where it is too late. By the time the now "enlightened man" finds out the truth about what he is involved in, the position, prestige and money associated with his position in the organization makes him oblivious to the fact that

**he has damned his soul to the devil. He made a pledge of himself and his children to the spirit of Hiram Abiff—the devil!**

You are no longer married to him, right? Do you still have his name? You cannot drive the spirit yet because he has legal ground through the name to come into your life. Legally you divorced him but the open door would be the name. Even if you drive away the spirit, it will keep coming back because the name is still a legal and spiritual connection of the two of you. You are still tied to him by his name that you answer. Until the day that you get rid of his name, you will find that from time to time you will contend with the Freemasonry spirit. When you give him back his name, then you can tell the spirit to pack up and go and you should then renounce every covenant you made with that spirit by virtue of your marriage and through his name. You can petition God to bring your children to the place where they can know Him and then renounce the covenant that their dad made on their behalf with the Hiram Abiff spirit. Meanwhile, His grace covers them.

***Question #6 Cont'd****: Do you think that I should discourage them from having a relationship with him then?*

***Mary's Answer****:* **No. The reason is because you will bring a curse on them if you separate them from their dad. God said in Malachi that the heart of the father is to be turned to the son and**

**the heart of the son to the father and if not, He would smite the earth with a curse. So, it is not in their best interest to keep their father out of their lives.**

*Mary Asks: Are they receptive to the things of the Lord?*

## *Student's Reply:* Yes.

**You can pray with them; they can renounce the covenant their dad made with Hiram Abiff and they can say no to Freemasonry and ask Jesus to be Lord of their lives. You can pray for the Lord to keep the spirit away from you until the day you legally change your name back to what you had before. Most women do not know this – either you are married to somebody or you are not. If you are divorced from someone and you keep the name, the spirit of the person has a right to come and go in your life. When you go to sleep at night, that spirit can come into your house and do whatever it pleases at any time. It has a legal ground – you are still part of that man through the name. A name is a very powerful thing.**

There was a lady who was divorced that I knew and I had told her that she needed to giver her ex-husband his name back but she never took it seriously. One day, I was spending the night at her house and when everyone in the house went to bed, an extremely tall spirit in the form of her ex-husband (taller than s five story building) took one step from the street and was right smack in the center of the house. It declared that it had legal grounds to come and go as he pleased and he went into one of the bedrooms. When I woke up I tried to tell her, she did not receive it so I left her alone. Names are legal grounds that connect ex-spouses even years after their divorce.

Also, I recently received a wristwatch as a gift from a friend of mine who have been separated from her husband for about three years but not yet divorced. When I went to sleep that night, the spirit in her husband came into my house to demand the wristwatch! It told me that woman and all that she owns belong to him. Because your spouse would still have spiritual claim to you and your properties, you cannot just walk away from a marriage and think that everything has been taken care of by your walking away.

Coming back to you sister, if I tell you that we can pray your ex-husband's (Hiram Abiff) spirit away when you are still keeping his name, I will be lying to you. As long as you keep his name, the spirit can fight off any man that would be interested in marrying you in the future. If your ex-husband is a possessive person, his spirit can keep other men away from you. Also, by keeping his name, you would still be subject to the things that go on in his life and in his family. They can still try to come against you through his name. If you do not want to keep dealing with issues from him and his family, then you have to get rid of his name so that you are no longer counted as a member of his family. As long as you are still part of him through the name, then whatever he is fighting in his family you will fight as well because of the name.

## *Mary Prays for Student.*

### *Repeat After Me:*

"Father God, in the Name of the Lord Jesus, I repent of every covenant that I made with the spirit of Freemasonry by virtue of the marriage covenant with __ _____ and I ask for forgiveness. I also repent for not knowing that the covenant was in place in my life. Now that I know, I repent of it, I condemn the covenant and I say that it is an abomination unto me and I ask that you forgive me, forgive my children and I ask that you deliver me and my children from the spirit of Freemasonry. I ask that you be a wall of fire between me and _____ and all his activities that are Freemasonry based. I say that the blood of Jesus is now between him and I in this area. Father, let the blood of Jesus and the cross of Jesus also be between him and the children in this area. As a parent over these children, I decree "no" to the spirit of Freemasonry over my children in Jesus' Name and over their children's children to the last generation. Free Masonry, I command you to go out of my life and my children's lives in Jesus' Name. Amen."

## Prayer: (Repentance)

"Father, in the Name of the Lord Jesus Christ, I thank you for revealing to her the root cause of divorce in her family. Father we forgive whoever was the first person to put away their spouse in her family in Jesus' Name. We ask that you forgive the person. I forgive the person for unleashing against us the spirit of divorce. I forgive the person for his or her selfishness in breaking up a home contrary to your will. Father, I ask that you forgive all my family members and remove the curse of divorce from our lives. Father, I ask you to protect my children that they will not suffer from the hand of this spirit. Father, I thank you in the Name of Jesus that your Word says that if the unbelieving husband should leave, I should let him leave. Therefore, I allowed him to leave and I say that my marriage covenant with him is now over. Father, I choose to give him back his name so that you can shut the door that he represents against me in Jesus' Name. Amen".

***Question #7:*** *I just wanted to share as one of the ladies came up about sanctifying the home. Several years ago I got saved and I went up to a convention at Rod Parsley's church and I came back full of the presence and the power of God and I remember the Holy Spirit had me going through my home to sanctify it. I started first with my husband's room and then I went to my daughter's room and when I went in my daughter's room there was a force that was so strong and I had my husband read Psalm 91; my daughter was just crying out. And in that force, I busted my knee on the side of her bed and my knee was swollen but God had me go down to the basement to every room in the house, just walking and just praying* *out and I went also to the back, onto the deck, open the garage door and let out whatever what was in the house. So I realized then how important it was to sanctify my house. But I just wanted to know if there's anything else that I can do now, just with the information you're sharing, to make sure that my house stays that way.*

**<u>*Mary's Answer:*</u> You have to sanctify your home from time to time because there are some people who come to visit and sometimes they carry what I told you about before—lingering spirits. Even phone calls that come into your home and television, voices that speak into your home. There are some people that carry spirits of infirmities and when they speak, their voices release whatever they are suffering from into your home. These people can release insomnia, unrest, sickness and diseases into your home. You have to terminate the visitation of such people after they leave your home because if you don't, you would find their spirit in your couch or somewhere in your home lingering. You have to get rid of them spiritually. Have you ever had a conversation with someone and then you are sitting down hours later and the conversation tries to keep replaying in your mind? This happens after you have a conversation with a person that carries the spirit of occult. Conversations with them are usually hard to shut off because the spirit of occult wants to keep it going. It might even go into your dream and begin to play out there. Whenever you talk to such**

**people, know that you have to always bring your encounter with them under the blood of Jesus and officially end every conversation with them so it does not continue while you are trying to rest or into your dream.**

From time to time, sanctify your home and pray and praise the Lord in your home. Periodically anoint your home and cancel the assignments sent against you and your home. For me, on the last day of every month, I thank the Lord for that month and the beginning of the first day of every month, I dedicate that month to the Lord and everything He's going to do and I cancel everything that was sent against me. I decree good things upon me for that month and then use that opportunity to sanctify my home and speak a Word of blessing upon my home.

**_Question #8:_** *Do you always think about ending the visit when someone comes to your house?*

**_Mary's Answer:_** **We used to have meetings at my house and I would bring the meetings to an end each time. I would say:**
"Father I thank you in the Name of the Lord Jesus that this meeting is now over; I now end the meeting spiritually. Until we meet again, there shall be no evil attempt to continue the meeting and I shall not be seeing myself in an evil classroom. Until the Lord brings us together again for His purpose, nobody shall come to me in an evil way or in an evil setting, in Jesus' Name."

**Prayer to terminate visits by people who carry evil spirits:**
*"Father God, in the Name of Jesus, I thank you that _____ came to visit me and I decree that the visitation is now over. Until she comes to visit me again, no spirit shall linger in my home through him or her. Whatever is not of you cannot stay. I do not give permission to any evil spirit to stay in my house. I plead the blood of Jesus over my house. Do this also even with phone calls. Until I talk to _____ again, I shall not be hearing their voice in my head or in my sleep contrary to the will of the Lord."*

**When you do this, you will not have their voices playing over and over in your head. The Lord usually allows me to know who carries those spirits so every time they call me, especially if they are members of my family, as soon as I finish talking to them, I would end the conversation spiritually.**

*"Father, in Jesus' Name, we thank you for everything you have taught us. We thank you for your presence here. Thank you Lord for helping us to put to practice those things you have revealed and imparted to us. We thank you for the honor and the privilege of being in your classroom and we give you all the glory. We say that this knowledge is not by might, nor power, it is by your Spirit and to you be all the glory in the Name of Jesus. Amen."*

***Note:*** *Remember that this book is from an actual classroom teaching.*

251

# Conclusion

I have presented the materials in this book in a way that is easy for even a new Christian to understand. My goal was to outline the key principles concerning evil spirits, their origin, their activities and how to discern and expel them. I also answered one of the most frequently asked question, "Can a Christian Have a Demon?"

My desire is that you know the truth for yourself because the Lord said that, **"Ye shall know the truth and the truth shall <u>make</u> you free"** (John 8:32). This is neither the time nor age for any Christian to be ignorant of the wiles (devices) of the devil. Demonic activities are real and we cannot pretend that they are not. The devil and his evil spirits are our enemies. They are out to harm us but the Lord has given us the authority and power to rebuke them, to bind them and to cast them out. We must be willing to use the power.

Scriptures tell us that **the earnest expectation of all of creation is the manifestation of the sons of God** (Romans 8:19). All of creation is waiting for us (the Church of Jesus Christ) to arise and take our place and demonstrate the wisdom and power of God here on earth. There is spiritual wickedness on earth and we are the soldiers of the Lord sent to root out the rebels. Creation itself is waiting for us to spring into action and destroy the spiritual wickedness currently going on in the nations.

The devil is no longer in charge of the earth. **The Lord Jesus Christ is now Lord of all** and He has commanded us to go and preach the Gospel to every creature. A great part of preaching the Gospel as the Lord demonstrated is casting out the evil spirits that hold people bound to false religions, sexual immoralities, lying, covetousness, greed, love of money, pride, strive, unforgiveness and acts of wickedness such as rape and murder. The great commission from the Lord in **Mark 16:15-17** is:

> *"Go ye into all the world, and preach the gospel to every creature. He that believeth and is baptized shall be saved; but he that believeth not shall be damned. And these signs shall follow them that believe; <u>In my name shall they cast out devils</u>; they shall speak with new tongues..."*

Let us obey the Lord by being willing to confront evil spirits. The Lord also commanded us **to occupy until He comes**. This means that we are to displaced the evil spirits and take over their strongholds for the Lord till He comes.
God bless you.

# Bibliography

Erskine, Noel Leo.  From Garvey to Marley Rasta-fari Theology, University Press of Florida, State Uni-vesity System. USA. 2005.

# TO HIS GLORY PUBLISHING COMPANY, INC.

463 Dogwood Dr. Lilburn, GA. 30047, U.S.A (770)458-7947

## Order Form for Bookstores in the USA

Order Date: ...........................................................

Order Placed By: ...........................................................     By fax: ...........................

Address: ...........................................................     By phone: ...........................

City ........................... ST/ZIP ...........................     Terms: ...........................

Phone#: ...........................................................

Email: ...........................................................     Discount: ...........................

Purchase Order#: ...........................................................

**Return Policy**: Within 1 Year but not before 90 days

### Title and ISBN#

| Price | Quantity | List Price |
|---|---|---|
| | | |
| | | |
| | | |
| | | |
| | | |
| | | |
| | | |
| | | |
| | | |
| Shipping Method: | | |
| Media | | |
| UPS | | |
| FedEx | | |
| Other (please describe) Total Price: | Total Quantity: | |

Ship To Address:                          Bill To Address:

TO HIS GLORY PUBLISHING COMPANY, INC (770) 458-7947 Use Only - Billing Information